Michael Kavan
Copthall.

# WALES
## & the Welsh
### TREVOR FISHLOCK

CASSELL · LONDON

CASSELL & COMPANY LTD
35 Red Lion Square, London WC1R 4SJ
Sydney, Auckland
Toronto, Johannesburg

First published 1972

I.S.B.N. 0 304 93858 0

Printed in Great Britain by
The Camelot Press Ltd, London and Southampton
F. 372

# Contents

# Preface

I came to Wales as a stranger in the last month of 1968 and,
although I always try to keep an open mind whenever I go into
a new place or situation, I brought, inevitably, some of the
stranger's preconceptions. Wales was largely a *terra incognita*: I
knew nothing of its history, little of its geography. At school we
were told that 'Wales = coal' and we hurried to fit in Scotland
and Ireland before the bell went. I knew nothing of the princes,
poets, writers, fighters and other big men of Wales. I knew little
of one of the great human stories of history: the explosive
growth of the coal field in the south, and its decline. As I drank
my first drink in Wales I realized that my knowledge of the
politics and personalities and the currents and background of
Welsh society was merely surface, that I could not even pro-
nounce the name of the pub I was in. I decided to keep my
mouth shut and listen.

I have been fortunate in that my work has been an explora-
tion of a society and a country. It has taken me on frequent
journeys to every part of Wales, to listen to people of every
view, to observe and to interpret events.

These are fascinating times to be in Wales because, apart
from the important economic struggle, there is a conflict which,
in various and intricate ways, affects most of the people of
Wales. The Welsh-speaking minority are fighting to provide for
their language a valid and vigorous future existence, and in
doing so are struggling to retain their individuality against the
bullying uniformity of modern life.

This book, which I started two-and-a-half years after settling
in Wales, is not a guide book or a history, but I hope it will
serve as a guide to the events of one of the most interesting
decades in the history of Wales, to the social and historical
background, and to the feelings of those involved. Partly, it is
written for those who, like myself, have wanted to know more
of the people and the forces at work in Welsh life, and have

wondered about some of the facets of this sometimes mis-represented, often misunderstood country which, in a sense, is England's unknown neighbour. It sets out to answer many of the questions that I have been asking during the time I have lived and worked here—even the basic one 'Why are there so many Joneses?' led to a facet of social history and a rich humour previously unchronicled. Also, it gives Welsh people and Welsh exiles a stranger's eye view of their native country.

Sometimes people express surprise that I enjoy being in Wales. Well, Wales may not be an island, but it is different from England; it is not perfect, but I like it for its faults rather than despite them. I like its separate character, its sense of community, continuity and history, the stimulation created by the conflict of identity. On all levels of life in Wales there is a current of argument of a kind not found in England. With all this, and a beautiful landscape and a mixture of accents and another language, there is more than enough for a kind of magic.

I appreciate that the Welsh love of genealogy insists on a brief analysis of my blood. My grandfather, like so many Englishmen at the end of the last century, came to work in South Wales as a miner. My grandmother was Welsh and my father was born here but, like so many others, he left in the depression because there was no work. I suppose, therefore, that I am a Welsh quadroon, and, through being here, I have experienced the mild sensation of a reconnection with a rather tenuous root in the most civilized place I have ever lived in.

*Pant-y-questa,*
*Glamorgan.*

# Acknowledgements

I wish to thank, and admit an unpayable debt, to all of those who have given me so much of their time to talk over the endlessly fascinating subject of Wales and the Welsh, and I would like, too, to acknowledge the sources of some of the quotations in this book. All my impressions of Wales have been gained in the years I have been reporting Welsh affairs for *The Times*, and a few fragments and phrases originally appeared in articles I wrote for my newspaper. Mr Saunders Lewis has allowed me to reproduce parts of his BBC radio lecture on February 1962, and I have drawn on the English translation by Elizabeth Edwards (the first English translation of the lecture), published in the magazine *Planet* in 1971. Colin Palfrey's poem, two of John Jenkins's letters and Dr Bobi Jones's personal note on Welsh also first appeared in *Planet* in 1971. Judge Watkin Powell and Mr Ted Rowlands have allowed me to quote from the important lectures they gave in the autumn of 1971. Newspaper quotations are acknowledged in the text. I have also used an observation by Gwyn Thomas in *A Welsh Eye* (Hutchinson, 1964) and parts of Professor T. J. Morgan's thoughtful summary of the problems of Welsh language teaching published in *Aspects of Primary Education* (Schools Council/Evans/Methuen Educational). The chapter title 'Where toil the Cymry' is from a poem by W. H. Davies, whose collected poems are published by Jonathan Cape. The title 'We are a musical nation' is, of course, from Dylan Thomas's *Under Milk Wood*. Thanks to friends who encouraged and to Rhys David, David Lewis, David Meredith and Dafydd Williams, who went through the script and gave helpful advice, and to Angela, my wife, who typed, far into many nights, every word.

# A note on the language

Every year thousands of people set out to learn Welsh by way of the radio, or evening class, or in school. One of the problems they encounter is mutation—the fact that Welsh dislikes sharp edges and alters and softens certain consonants at the beginnings of words according to the preceding words. Thus, the word for 'Wales' is *Cymru*, pronounced kumree, but 'Welcome to Wales' is *Croeso i Gymru*. *Tad* means 'father' but *fy nhad* is 'my father'. Mutation is governed by laws and when Welsh is used within an English text the question of mutation leads to learned arguments. I have had to make choices in this matter and my aim has always been the achievement of clarity.

# 1 Land of their fathers

It is true that Welshmen sing like angels, play Rugby Union football like princes, hew coal like heroes, live in thin valleys, fry a seaweed called laver bread with their breakfast bacon, pray in chapels, compete and dress up at *eisteddfodau*, speak an ancient language, write poetry, pluck harps, call daughters Blodwen, talk at length in committees and become teachers. Some have no doubt done all of these things. But clichés die hard. Each country has its image compounded of part-truths and the Welsh caricature, like a fairground hall of mirrors, does not give a true reflection. It is as accurate as the pictures of Englishmen as pinstriped, cricket-going, old-chapping, fair-playing, bowler-hatted, four o'clock tea addicts, the French as bereted, garlic-scented, snail-biting boudoirists; the Scots as haggis-piping, plaided, och-ayeing, wee-drappie-drinking skin-flints. The way that some people talk you would think there was pithead winding gear at the top of St Mary's Street in Cardiff and files of miners singing, for heaven's sake, as they tramp to work à la *How Green Was My Valley*.

The real Wales is an attractive enigma. It is not too difficult to find bits of it that fit the image, but it is a great deal more than pits, choirs, Taffies and a way of speaking, and all the fragments of popular belief that are partly true but amount in sum to a fiction.

Whatever I say about Wales will not necessarily be agreed by any two Welshmen. Wales is a meld of differences and there is a tradition of argument. Shout yes in a street in Wales, goes an old commentary, and a dozen people will shout back no. Wales is nothing if not a land of contrasts and contradictions and Welshmen themselves sometimes seem to change like the mutating nouns of their marvellous language and are as hard to pin down as darting sewin in a Carmarthenshire stream. Wales, though small, cannot be tidily parcelled. Just as you think you have the picture right somebody gives the kaleidoscope a nudge and moves the bits.

I

But there can be no dispute with the physical facts with which I start. Wales is a distinct entity, a mainly beautiful land, wild, damp, dramatic and mountainous, segmented by fine rivers. It is a symphony of great, gaunt, fortress peaks, stark crags and black wet cliffs, rolling hills, the haunt of lonely hunting birds, jetting falls, silent and indigo lakes, secret *cwms* and warm, green valleys. Wales, as a nation, endures: the geography has moulded the people and has been fundamental in ensuring their survival as a distinct people.

And when Welshmen speak as if Wales were the ante-room to paradise you cannot quarrel with them. If you fail to be stirred by Welsh landscape you will never get to heaven, for you have no soul. Gaze at the quilt of Carmarthenshire from the Black Mountain; at the estuary of the matchless Mawddach; at the magic coasts of Gower and Lleyn; at lonely, grand Plynlimon, down whose slopes bubble five infant rivers; at the fair country of the Vale of Glamorgan, braising on a heavy-hot day; at the skewbald skies and aspects of purple mountains in the north; at the beaches and cliffs in the west— and you will have an inkling of why their landscape is to them a song and inspiration.

But Wales is also industrial and bruised. Men have dug into it for its coal, slate and ores. Romans scratched it for its gold. Welshmen carved slate from the mountains to put a roof over Britain's head and dug out coal for the warships, the traders and the great industries. They gave their lives and health toiling, in the words of the poet W. H. Davies 'deep in sunless pits, and emptying all their hills to warm the world'. In parts, therefore, Wales is hideously scarred. But, jerked from apathy and acceptance of ugliness by the unspeakable tragedy of Aberfan, Welshmen are clearing up the heartless messes of the epoch of coal and are putting back the flowers in the valleys.

This is a country full of castles and fortresses, for it was once the fightingest part of Britain and, still, it has not been put down entirely. It is chapel-garrisoned, too, for Wales was once a preachers' province and has said and sung its generous share of prayers in piety, desperation and grief. In terms of sheer prayer-hours it must have a handsome credit balance in heaven.

It is a country that has known many sadnesses through social upheaval, blood on the coal and industrial bitterness. It is a country of about 8000 square miles in which live more than 2,700,000 people, one twentieth of the population of Britain. It is a principality, a title that has only ceremonial significance. The best and hottest black-diamond coal in the world and cool, soft water are among its riches; and among its exports are its people, many of them talented, for Wales started the brain drain a good four centuries ago.

Curiously, its history, fabulous stories, its character and great men are barely known in its neighbour, conqueror and landlord, England: in the same way that people in big-city flats live under the same roof for years but know little of each other.

Curiously, too, many Welsh schools have traditionally taught very little Welsh history. Which is sad because, as Edmund Burke remarked, people will not look forward to posterity, who never look backward to their ancestors. In Wales, history in school has nearly always meant English history. And if those Englishmen who come into contact with Welsh history dislike it, it is probably because it is, in parts, a saga in which the Englishman always seems to feature as the baddy.

It is a country where the great national events are poetry championships and Rugby football matches and the people all but canonize the star poets and the star players. Its capital city of Cardiff has a Colosseum dedicated to Rugby football, where Englishmen are sacrificed on Saturday afternoons. The city has, too, a famous park of administration, learning and roses, a campus of white and columned buildings rising from kempt turf. Like many capitals, this one does not reflect the full flavour of the country it figureheads. But it has a stirring motto beneath its escutcheon—*y Ddraig Goch ddyry cychwyn*: the Red Dragon leads the way. And one day, when it has solved frustrating problems, it may be a very fine city.

In the eighth century King Offa of Mercia ordered the building of the ditch and earthwork which runs 168 miles from North Wales to the Severn shore in the south. Offa's Dyke was not a defence, it was a political and racial boundary, as much a recognition of Wales as a device to stop Welsh cowboys rustling English cattle. 'You keep on your side of it, we'll keep on ours.' The border between England and Wales which roughly follows

3

Offa's demarcation line is an ancient ditch between two cultures and Wales retains its old position as the stronghold in the
west, an independent land, a land apart. In the Welsh language
it is called *Cymru* and it is the home of a people whose ancestors
were the original Britons: warriors, clever and cultured. They
did not flee here, treading the shadows of invaders and finding
mountain boltholes: they grew here and built their nation and
the mountains were their fortress. The word Welsh is an old one
derived from the Anglo-Saxon *wealeas* meaning foreign. But in
their own language the people of Wales call themselves the
*Gymry*, a word that conveys warmth and strength and means
brothers or comrades.

The stranger will soon know he is in a different country and
by far more than the formality of the sign by the road, *Croeso i
Gymru*: Welcome to Wales. After a while he will detect a change
in the atmosphere and then he will begin to take in the differences, the intangibles that are part of the charm of Wales.

He will observe that the countryside has a distinctive flavour:
the mountains have the sweep and drama I have mentioned,
and, in the industrialized south-east, in the rough fan of valleys
just wide enough for Rugby but not for cricket, there are the
sights which slot into the preconceived picture. Fifty working
coalmines and scores of derelict ones, countless dirty tips, the
bashed land, the industrial junk, the snaking terraces piton'd
to the hillsides, pinafored wives holystoning steps, chapels,
vast and gaunt pubs, many of them boarded up, the miners'
mossy *pissoirs* on the roadsides, the little corner shops: Jones-
Grocer, Jones-Baker, Jones-Draper. It is scruffy, certainly, and
depressing in parts, because men have kicked beauty in the
teeth. But it is often homely and worn and warm, not always
unforgivably ugly. Even the battered Rhondda is still, like its
people, rugged, stubborn and grand.

In the valleys the newcomer will occasionally see small heaps
of coal lying at the roadside. This is the coalminers' concessionary coal and, when it is tipped from the lorry, it obviously has
to be moved quickly because it is in the way. Some colliers
loathe more than anything else the task of humping the coal
through the house to the back yard. One day, exhausted after a
night shift and desperate for sleep, a miner went to his bed after

4

instructing his wife he was not to be disturbed on any account. He had not long drifted into sleep when his wife burst into the room.

'Evan, Evan,' she cried, shaking him vigorously. He opened one eye. 'The king is dead.'

'Thank God it's only that,' Evan said, turning over. 'I thought the coal had been delivered.'

The sheep are everywhere in Wales: there are more than six million of them. Sometimes you can see the flocks being driven along dusty lanes by men on horseback, with Black Bobs darting down low to head off stragglers. The sheep are plump and clean in the hills, random specks of wool on the high mountains, dead by the roadside sometimes, doleful and dog-eared in the streets of the valley towns where they plunder the gardens and mooch and rummage about in the back yards.

'I always order Welsh lamb or mutton in restaurants,' a friend said at lunch, 'in the hope that I'll get to the woolly bastard that keeps tipping my dustbin over.'

There are many outward manifestations of a country with its special identity. Distinctive accents, of course (and varying ones so that you will soon be able to distinguish between the southern accent and the northern one); place-names apparently full of consonants, villages with solid and plain chapels rather than fancy-fenestered churches; Post Office vans inscribed *Post Brenhinol* as well as Royal Mail; the stone circles of the *gorsedd* of bards all over the country, like little Stonehenges. There are distinctive Christian names, as if to compensate for somewhat drab surnames. Men are called Alcwyn, Aneirin, Dafydd, Emrys, Emyr, Elwyn, Eifion, Emlyn, Elystan, Elfed, Elfyn, Gwilym, Guto, Gwyn, Hywel, Idris, Iorwerth, Owen, Llion, Lyn, Meirion, Rhodri and Rhys. Women are called Bronwen, Lowri, Mair, Meleri, Myfanwy, Megan, Meinir, Sian, Rhon-wen and Rhiannon. In the north and west, Welsh is the every-day language and in some remote parts are a few scores of very elderly people who are the remnants of an old Wales, all but vanished, and speak only Welsh. They know nothing of the language they call *Saesneg* and most of us call English.

Strangers should not expect to find women in rural Wales wearing long skirts, shawls and tall black hats as some of the books and postcards have led them to believe. The so-called national costume of Wales was a nineteenth-century invention for the benefit of tourists.

The newcomer will see that, rather oddly, a lot of road signs have been obliterated by green paint, or covered with stickers, and he may wonder why. Also that the Welsh, strangely for a nation not normally given to extrovert displays and symbolism, have recently produced a strain of human-fly slogan writers. Bridges, walls and convenient blackboards of rock have stark symbols painted on them and slogans like Free Wales from the English, *Cymraeg! Cofia Dryweryn*, Gwynfor! Free Wales, Home Rule and *Cymru am byth.* . . .

*Cymru am byth* means Wales for ever and, although it is often seen in graffiti and on souvenir mugs, plaques and tea towels, it is for many people in Wales much more than a superficial slogan. It is a clue to an unselfconscious pride. The story goes that once, when a tide of national feeling was running through Wales, and even scoffers were sporting Welshness like new overcoats, the sober-suited congregation in a valley chapel one Sunday morning, spent the service facing a neatly-lettered placard. It read Wales for Ever. After the congregation had departed down the street, and the hymn-warmed air had drifted upward, a deacon confessed to the minister that, taken by the mood of the times, he had been the author of the poster. The minister conceded privately that he approved of the placard's sentiment but, on the ground that it was not, or not quite, a religious statement, judged it unsuitable for the chapel. He left for his lunch of Welsh lamb. That evening he and the congregation returned to see the placard, not removed, but amended: Wales for Ever—and Ever, Amen.

I think most Welshmen love Wales more than most English-men love England. Or perhaps it just appears that way. Welsh-men are not so inhibited, upper lips not so stiff, when it comes to expressing love of their native land. Englishmen keep such emotions locked up in a safe, Welshmen on a handy shelf with the rest of their feelings. Englishmen permit themselves the occasional fix of fervour, a lump in the throat at, say, the last night of the Proms and goose pimples at some great ceremonial or national event when the Union flag flutters in the breeze.

6

But Wales is constantly in the songs and poetry, books and sermons, talk and graffiti of Welshmen. Love of mother-*Cymru* is etched in the soul. 'We have a joke, my friends and I,' a man, admittedly a nationalist, said. 'When we meet we say: Let's see if we can go ten minutes without talking about Wales.' Englishmen take for granted the prestige of their country and their ubiquitous language, their heritage and the security of admired values and the way of life. Welshmen do not have that luxury.

In England *God save the Queen* is a noted emptier of cinemas. See, depending on the circumstances, how the people flee, or fidget or mumble or wait in embarrassed silence, as it is played. And how many know more than the first verse? It is exactly the same in Wales—for *God save the Queen.*

But at the first notes of *Hen Wlad fy Nhadau* (*Land of my Fathers*), the anthem written in 1856 by two Pontypridd weavers, Evan and John James, and transfused into the country's soul, note the difference. See how erect the people stand for the song that says so much for the way they feel about Wales, how high their heads are held, what a fine thunder their voices make, how their eyes dew.

It is true that in varying circumstances people sing the anthem for different motives. The crowd at Cardiff Arms Park, the temple of Rugby football, swaying sparkle-eyed to the roared-out anthem, are involved in a great communal experience, in the electric unity of tribalism, and their excitement will evaporate. In any case many of them do not know the meaning of the Welsh words of the anthem that they learned parrot-fashion at school or chapel or on grandfather's knee. Yet there is an element in their singing of affirming their identity. And whatever the reasons for singing the anthem with such enthusiasm it cannot be a simple matter of the Welsh having the infinitely better tune.

I cannot imagine the English going in for festivals of red roses, Union Jacks and patriotic music on St George's Day, even if they can remember when it is. But in Wales, upon St David's Day, the first of March, there is such a welling of *hiraeth*, nostalgia, such a harvest of King Alfred daffodils, such a burgeoning of leeks, such a roasting of celebratory dinners, such

7

a toasting at parties, such a tinkling of harps, such a flap of Red Dragons, such an ectoplasmic outpouring from BBC Wales, such a roar of *Men of Harlech*, you would think the people would suffocate from pride or, at the very least, bring Owain Glyndwr, the mediaeval warrior prince and hero, French sword in hand, golden lion on his tunic breast, down from the mountains.

Still, it must be admitted that some of the people who go around merrily *Cymru am byth*-ing on St David's Day are little more than one-day-a-year Welshmen who store away their pride in identity and bring it out for the day and wear it, with sweet hypocrisy, like a hat.

A strong pride, however, is genuine enough in many of the people of Wales. Thus the man who won the bardic crown at the 1970 national *eisteddfod* said at his press conference, with a simple and unselfconscious pride: 'I am a Welshman, thank God.' There is a greetings card on sale in Wales intended for couples who have just had a baby. It depicts a pram with a tiny hand peeping out waving a Red Dragon flag. 'Congratulations,' is the message. 'Another little Welshman!' There are Welshmen of my acquaintance whose love of their land is uncrushable, who would sing its praises even on the rack. And I have a suspicion that some of them expect to find that heaven lies somewhere in Snowdonia and that Welsh is the *lingua franca* there. Indeed, they might opt for the other place if God turned out to be an Englishman after all.

Yet one of them told me recently: 'It is true that I love my country but if there is such a thing as reincarnation I hope I will come back an Englishman. To be spared the neuroses and hang-ups of Welshness, to stop worrying about the threats to the nation and the heritage, to stop all this self-analysis, to stop adopting a self-justifying and defensive attitude would be a release from a burden.'

Now many people in Wales will know exactly what he means and others will not have the faintest idea except that he sounds a suitable case for treatment. His remark, however, is a clue to the fact that Wales today is a land of some torment and much argument, self-examination and bitter cross-argument. Many of the people are involved in a conflict of identity.

They are constantly having to face the question of their Welshness, to decide what that means, to make up their minds whether
they feel Welsh or British, to decide where they should place
their loyalty and what their commitment to Wales should be.
Others, more certain of their Welshness, are concerned to
maintain their separate Welsh identity, to ensure that, in the
symbiosis with England, it is not swamped. The conflict is an
emotional and instinctive one and a large part of it is expressed
in what is known as 'the language question'. In one sense, far
from everyone being united behind one great Red Dragon,
Wales is a split-level country. There is Welsh Wales and English
Wales, or, if you prefer, not-so-Welsh Wales. They are not two
distinct factions, a dangerous over-simplification, they are like
rock strata which have slipped along a fault-line. The frontier
cannot be drawn on a map because the edges are fuzzy and
frequently changing: it is partly a matter of language, partly of
background, partly of attitude and instinct and emotion. Because it is Wales it is not a question of black-and-white distinction: it is a Celtic rainbow of softly melding greys. At times you
have to be careful in the use of the simple word 'Welsh' because,
whatever it means in England, the word has a number of
slightly different meanings, in differing contexts, within Wales.
It may mean simply the inhabitants of Wales, but it might
mean the Welsh-speakers, or it might be applied to individuals
who fit a particular notion of Welshness.

If you watch the correspondence columns of the newspapers
in Wales, or incline an ear to discussions, you will see or hear
the plea: 'Why on earth can't we put an end to all this Welsh
and English squabbling? Why don't we in Wales just agree that
we are British and be done with it?' Now this will strike many
people as a sensible suggestion, as a facing up to facts. It will
strike many others as an outrageous heresy. Because British
means English and a large number of Welsh people feel, are,
and want to remain, different from the English.

Wales is nine-tenths a conquered country and the un-
conquered bit is not territory but the character of the people
and the qualities of the Welsh way of life. These have survived
centuries of invasion, infiltration, legal and cultural garrotting,
educational repression, scorn and apathy. So that, while only

9

two Pullman hours from London, fifty miles from Birmingham and with Liverpool leaning on its right shoulder, this land of Wales retains a grip on its separate character, its air of independence and its heritage. If you travel north or west of the Black Mountain, outrider of the Brecon Beacons, the Welsh way of life is part of the weave and the enigma and the magic of Wales.

Hundreds of years after the battleaxing, town-burning, treaty-making and glowering across the border between the English and the Welsh, and four centuries after the Act of Union brought Wales more or less to heel, the Welsh people still feel they have suffered conquest. This is not romance. The national memory is very long and retentive and conquest has left the Welsh, whether thoroughly anglicized or not, feeling vulnerable and sensitive about their nationality. A certain thinness of the skin and inferiority complex is one of the well-known marks of a subject people. The people of Welsh Wales, the minority, often feel pushed into a corner and see their own values besieged on all sides, their language crumbling. Their anxiety to maintain their special identity, and all the things they hold fundamental, is at the root of the conflict and struggling in Wales today. Many of those Welsh people who have lost the old language and direct contact with their heritage feel guilty or resentful or at least uncomfortable about it.

On a people-to-people basis there is no hostility towards the English. This is not to say that there is in some quarters no resentment of English influences. Targets for criticism are television ('brainwashing our children') and the buyers of weekend cottages ('sapping the Welsh life from the countryside'). But these are the manifestation of more fundamental feelings and forces at work in Wales today. And some of it is, anyway, channelled to a humorous outlet: 'Keep Wales Tidy', says a popular car sticker, 'dump your rubbish in England'.

Sometimes you might hear someone use a sharp 'English!' as an insult, but it is generally applied to a Welshman who has annoyed by getting a bit above his station or has taken to speaking with a plum in his mouth. A section of the people of Wales has a ripe dislike of British authority and insists on calling the British government the English, or London, government. But whatever the view about English and English-American influences on Welsh values, there is no abrasion of importance between Welsh people and English people. But there is certainly abrasion and sometimes bitterness between the people of Welsh Wales who want to retain and encourage traditional values and those among the anglicized Welsh who are content to regard Wales as simply another part of Britain.

To many people in the industrialized south-eastern part of Wales, where three-quarters of the population lives, and along the border, the concept of identity and a way of life different from the English way is either doubtful or meaningless. In some parts Welshness has been all but obliterated. Even so, many people living in districts that became anglicized long ago still feel Welsh, as distinct from English, and are proud of vestigial Welshness. 'How do you spell your name?' a reporter from London asked a Mr Davies at a press conference. 'With an E,' growled Mr Davies. 'The Welsh way.'

On the other hand there are still people who regard Welshness as a taint, still parents who send their children to school in England so that they will escape the Welsh language, still people who are embarrassed by their ability to speak Welsh. It is a hangover from the old days when Welsh had an inferior social status. In a pub, a Welshman watching the Welsh language news on television turned to me and said: 'They should be ashamed of themselves, talking like Pakistanis.' Two prejudices for the price of one. There are some who regard the manifestations of their native culture as 'all that Welsh nonsense' and the people of the Welsh-speaking areas as 'that lot in Druid Land'. Possession of the Welsh language does not necessarily mean that a man cares for it. I was surprised the first time I heard a Welsh-speaker say: 'The sooner we get rid of it and content ourselves with a useful international language, the better off we shall be.'

Welsh Wales, as I have remarked, has no firm frontier. Its people are everywhere, in rural cottages, industrial terraces and in the avenues of semi-detached houses in Cardiff: they are united, not because they are one side of a particular brook, but by a belief in their national identity and their common wish for its survival through the culture, language and values which are the component parts of the Welsh way of life. Although Welsh

11

Wales is everywhere it is naturally strongest in the country—in the western counties of Anglesey, Caernarvonshire, Merioneth, west Montgomeryshire, north Pembrokeshire, Cardiganshire and Carmarthenshire.

I don't think there are clear physical differences between the English and the Welsh. Stocky, dark-haired men are typical of one sort of Welshman, and tall, fair men are typical of another sort. Wales also has its special line in fair-haired women with the kind of wistful beauty you see in faded sepia photographs, and girls with dark and gypsy looks. But the real differences of course are in attitudes and character, the result of a different history and environment.

A German student gave me this impression: 'In my own country people are materialist, concerned very much with making money. English people are more tolerant, not so pushing and not so concerned with money. Here in Wales the people seem to be even more tolerant and even less concerned about material things.'

It was a generalization, of course, but a fair one, I think. Welsh people, particularly those in rural Wales, are, in the best sense of the word, amateurs. They like the things that money buys, but life has to mean a lot more than simply turning out products. And although I may be mistaking the cream for the milk, a fair measure of altruism is a characteristic of the people of Wales. They are sociable and community-minded. Their garden fences are more for talking over than for separation. Today they are not classless, but they are certainly far less class-conscious than the English. Nor are they hierarchical: the curious system in some large companies of awarding managers and directors their own lavatory could never have originated in Wales.

They are naturally courteous, easy going and given to procrastination, so that out-and-out men of action are not typically Welsh. They have a fairly strong pacifist streak and there are few military terms in their language. Where other people turn to fist and gun to solve problems, Welshmen form committees.

They have a deep interest in, and concern for, other people which has always shown itself in strong community spirit and welfare as well as in gossip and inquisitiveness. They are strongly radical and conservative, anxious to maintain the feeling for democracy which evolved through their small communities. Their sense of the importance of other people is allied to their absorbing interest in things of the mind.

I would say that the Welsh are the most welcoming and the least xenophobic people I have met. Their hospitality is marvellous and they are the fastest people in the world with the teapot, bread-saw and cake-knife. It is perfectly natural to Welsh people that the Wales Tourist Board should be known in the native language as *Bwrdd Croeso i Gymru*, which means Wales Welcome Board.

The Welsh are more naturally cultured than the English and have a greater love for education which does not spring simply from 'getting on' motives. Some of the aspects of the Welsh, which the cleric known as Gerald the Welshman wrote about in the twelfth century, after journeying through the country, have changed little in 800 years. 'Nature has given not only to the highest, but also to the inferior classes of the people of this nation, a boldness and confidence in speaking and answering, even in the presence of their princes and chieftains,' he wrote.

'These people being of a sharp and acute intellect, and gifted with a rich and powerful understanding, are more quick and cunning than the other inhabitants of a western clime. . . . In their rhymed songs and set speeches they are so subtle and ingenious that they produce ornaments of wonderful and exquisite invention.' Gerald also noted: 'As no nation labours more under the vice of jealousy than the Irish, so none is more free from it than the Welsh.'

The Welsh people have a long folk memory and a well-tuned sense of ancient heritage. Thus this advertisement in *The Times* in October of 1971:

In Memoriam—David III—Last ruling Prince of Wales of the Royal House of Gwynedd, gallant and heroic defender of his country's honour in her most tragic hour. Barbarously tortured and executed at Shrewsbury, October 3, 1283. '*A ddioddefws a orfu.*'—A.J.H.R.

13

I remember watching a rally at Cilmeri, in Breconshire, around a granite monument which marks the place where Llewelyn (or Llywelyn), a great Prince of Wales, was slain by the English in 1282. It was as if the prince, with whom perished much hope and vision, and dreams of independent Wales, had been hacked to death only a few years before. And in some parts of Wales you might think, from the way people talk, that Owain Glyndwr, who headed the glorious failure of a Welsh revival more than 500 years ago, had vanished but lately.

The old rhyme which goes 'Taffy was a Welshman, Taffy was a thief' is rather resented by the sensitive because, in the context of Welsh community life, serious crime is rare. The poaching of salmon and trout, however, is a different matter. Welshmen know that fish were put into rivers by God for men to catch, not just for the sport of Midlands Englishmen. The passing of the bulky parcel from poacher to customer, who may have been, on rare occasions in the past, the local policeman, is still a solemn ceremony in some remote inns.

Between the peoples of the south and the north of Wales there is a long-standing, but not serious, rivalry. Further away from English influences, and the product of a harder environment, north Walians appear more solemn and remote on the surface. 'They're bloody mountain men up there,' a south Walian said disparagingly in an authentic Cardiff accent which had the bite of a circular saw. The people in the south, who are much more of a mixture, suspect that the people of the north regard themselves as the 'real Welsh'. The northerners, for their part, tend to look on south Walians as a rather volatile lot. The accents of north and south, whatever the language, differ sharply. In the same way that a Devonian would have a little trouble keeping up with a Geordie in full spate, a Pembrokeshire man would have to concentrate to follow the words of a man speaking Welsh in a broad Anglesey accent.

One of the differences between north and south is in the sense of humour. In the north the humour is of a rather dour kind and there is a liking for solemn leg-pulling. In the south the people have a sharper humour and a flair for repartee.

In the village of Gwaelod-y-garth, near Cardiff, a man wanting an extra window in his cottage set to work with hammers and chisels, hacking away at the thick stone wall. It took him much longer than he had imagined. At the end of the day he was leaning exhausted, irritable and swearing softly beside the gaping hole when a passing villager asked brightly: 'What's the matter, Emlyn? Lost your key?'

In a Rhondda pub one Sunday morning the men in the public bar were dark-suited and sober-tied. A workman came in, to be gently scolded by the landlord for being in overalls on a Sunday. 'These are the clothes that do the work,' said the man, slapping down his money. 'These are the clothes that drink the beer.'

In a valley shop one morning an assistant noticed that his somewhat oppressive employer had a plaster on his nose.

'You're off on your holidays, then?' he asked, innocently.

'Holidays? What do you mean?'

'Oh, I thought you were off, seeing you had your trunk labelled ready.'

Welsh society did not develop in the manner of English society. The middle class, the aristocrats and the landed gentry drifted away when the administration of Wales was centralized in the Act of Union of 1536. The attractions of the London life drew them away and those who remained were not strong enough to provide social leadership. A middle class has emerged in Wales only relatively recently. The culture of Wales developed largely without support of the lords and manor house bosses and was a folk culture in the hands of the ordinary people, what, in Welsh, is known as the *gwerin*. This word is often translated as the working class, or the Welsh folk, but there is no neat equivalent in English because the word is a shorthand way of expressing the warmth and dignity and community spirit of the ordinary people.

Two hundred years ago the *gwerin* began to take to the ideals of nonconformity: the temperament of the people and the fact that the established church had largely failed in its duties made Wales ripe for religious revival. As the population expanded the Calvinistic Methodists, Congregationalists, Baptists, Wesleyan Methodists and Unitarians became the great power in the land. When people migrated from the country to the coal valleys in the south they naturally took their life-style with them and community life in the valleys was organized on rural lines with the chapel as the hub. The seventy years until the outbreak of the First World War were the golden age of the chapel movement. Most of the solid chapels which are a feature of villages throughout Wales date from this period. To the Welsh the Church of England represented the landowners, Toryism and Englishness and was therefore not relevant.

As the moulders of attitude and as places of learning, the chapels have been a great force in Welsh politics and education. In their heyday they were not just places of worship, they were the centres of small democracies. In them the people received education, learned to debate and administrate. They learned to explore their literature and to appreciate and write poetry. In chapels, too, there developed the tradition of choral singing. In bursts of *hwyl*, fervour, some congregations would sing hymns for a whole day, or even two or three, and the hymns would have dozens of verses. From about 1870 the male voice choir, the great mixed choirs and the tag of 'land of song', became a part of the Welsh image.

The chapels were also the foundation of the remarkable movement for education in Wales—and for growing social and political and national awareness and the pressure for reform. From this awareness grew the desire for those institutions which are badges of nationality as well as being pillars of national life: the university, the national museum and library, the *eisteddfod* and the capital city. Through the chapel movement the Welsh people kept a grip on their ancient identity. The Bible had been translated into Welsh in 1588 and this had the double effect of bestowing prestige on the language and ensuring its use. Its employment in religious life, and therefore community life and education, was a vital carapace against the effects of the Act of Union which made English the language of administration and courts. Had the Bible not been translated into Welsh the language would certainly have gone the way of others, like Cornish.

Cultural standards among the ordinary people have always been high. Today, still, a good music degree rates more prestige in some parts than a B.Sc. The Welsh of the countryman has usually been of a higher standard than the English of his counterpart in England. Indeed, the plain country chapel

Welsh, however old-fashioned, is often regarded as the best spoken Welsh (except by a few lofty scholars).

The relative classlessness of the culture has enabled Welsh people to communicate with each other in a fashion rare in England. Prize-winning poets at the *eisteddfodau*, the cultural *grand prix*, are not necessarily the literati. The winners are labourers, miners, roadmen and shepherds, as well as ministers of religion and teachers. A time when the sheets of metal at South Wales ironworks were covered with chalked *cywydd*, a fourteenth century verse form written in strict metre, is still remembered. And today books of poetry still sell better in Wales than in England and literary magazines have a greater relative circulation. In 1956 a Welsh miner left his collection of 400 Welsh-language prose and poetry books to the University of Wales. He had bought twenty-five a year for sixteen years.

The chapels gave much to Wales but for a time they took away something too. A lot of the merry music, the laughter and innocent fun shrivelled under the hard eyes of the preachers. The harp, the Welshman's precious harp, which had been central to his culture, was said to be the devil's instrument and the playing of it declined dramatically. A dire warning in a chapel said: 'Who Ever hear on Sunday Will Practis Playing at Ball it May Be before Monday The Devil Will Have you All.'

Like organized religion in many parts of the world, the non-conformist movement has declined dramatically in Wales. But if it is now a shrunken force, no longer the great power in the land, its emotional atmosphere and the values it set are in the background of the people of Wales. The fire-and-brimstone performances in the pulpit, the Sundays on which nothing happened that was not ordained by the chapel, are still a close memory for many. And in rural Wales—Welsh Wales—the chapel remains a considerable influence. Take, as an example, the matter of Sunday opening of pubs. Every seven years Welsh people vote on the question of whether they want the public houses in their particular county to close or open on Sundays. In the referendum of 1968 five of the thirteen counties voted to stay 'dry' on the Sabbath.

But, for the majority, although the chapel may be a background influence, the old-fashioned sanctions, the rigid and grey aspects, the Welsh Sunday, the chilling, warning sermons, the temperance fixation, are forgotten, ignored or meaningless. The carefree pint is as much a part of the Welsh social scene as in England. No beer tent has ever been pegged at the Royal National *Eisteddfod*, the great annual celebration of Welsh culture and affirmation of identity, yet many of its devoted supporters regard it as not simply an important cultural festival but an opportunity to meet friends, gossip and grip glasses in the nearest pubs. The clubs, rather than the pubs, rather than the chapels, are the social centres now in some valley communities. A few of them are well-equipped places that would look well enough in the West End of London. They grew up to fill the vacuum when the Welsh Sunday Closing Act was keeping the pubs closed on Sundays and the miners wanted their pints of mild to wash away the dust and the aches. The clubs offer not only drinking but welfare funds . . . as well as gambling, bingo, cabarets and girls wearing very little, sights that would have those pastors of old turning in their graves.

Economic and social changes have eroded the Welsh way of life. Massive depopulation (nearly half a million people quit Wales in the great depression), the rapid growth of English-language trade unionism, English immigration, the prestige and ubiquitousness of English, English–Welsh 'mixed marriages' and, of course, television, with its output of what its critics call 'anglo-american mediocrity', have battered away at Welsh values.

Today, as never before, the Welsh culture which is largely expressed through the Welsh language, is a culture facing a crisis of survival. The Welsh-speaking minority is fighting for a future existence. The 1961 census revealed that the number of people able to speak Welsh had declined to 656,000: twenty-six per cent of the population. It rang an alarm bell throughout Wales; the ringing has continued and grown stronger.

The concern and desperation that this situation has produced has made a section of the people of Wales regard themselves as people fighting a battle against powerful forces of oppression. Emotion has welled to a cry from the heart. Yet they cannot share their anguish with, or earn the sympathy of, many of their fellow Welshmen.

With the desperation and the anxiety there is sometimes an edge of anger, a tension of resentment and a sense of urgency. The passion which some people feel about the Welsh condition has to be seen to be believed. All this has produced the pattern of protest and agitation, demonstrations and court room scenes, which have become familiar in Wales in recent years and have made people outside vaguely aware of the issues. There was also a wild period of violence. A number of Welshmen came to the conclusion that the British government had to be made, in a dramatic manner, to understand that there was injustice, that Welsh values were being destroyed, that people felt very strongly. They convinced themselves that there was no alternative but to use gelignite to blow up buildings and pipelines. This was an episode in the struggle that ended in death for two young men and the maiming of a small boy.

The anxiety for the way of life is at the base of all the struggles over the valleys of Wales that are wanted by water authorities as reservoirs. Valley-drowning is an emotional subject . . . it evokes a picture of arrogant English bureaucrats marching into Wales, destroying a community that Wales can ill-afford to lose. The names of the valleys tend to be like names on a battle honours board.

It was the concern for values that produced the curious situation at the village school in Bryncroes, in Caernarvonshire, in 1970. The county council closed the school under a rationalization scheme which aimed to concentrate children in larger schools. But the local parents, feeling that their school was an integral part of their Welsh-speaking community, reopened it and ran it with the aid of some rebel teachers. In the end the council got its way by threatening legal action.

It is not surprising, I think, that there is sometimes an edge of chauvinism to the anger and frustration at the Welsh condition and the inroads on English influence, and letters to the newspapers occasionally adopt the tone of this one, in the *Guardian*, in June 1971:

'So many English people have already bought Welsh country cottages for weekend use only that it is now becoming increasingly difficult for young Welsh couples to set up home. . . . Every day more and more Welsh people are forced by economic

19

necessity to leave Wales because of a lack of work which successive London governments are just not attracting in any worthwhile quantity. . . . The great majority of people who have moved into Wales, moreover, contribute nothing to the glorious culture of Wales. If an Englishman moves to France to work, he would reasonably expect to have to learn to speak French. So it should be with Wales. . . .'

On much the same subject, this poem by Colin Palfrey:

A postcard in the window said it all:
'Wanted in Aberporth, a cottage, small,
2–3 bedrooms. Ready cash. Must hurry.'
And the address was somewhere 'nice' in Surrey.

Thus Welshmen sell their castles to the Crown,
Doffing their caps while noble valleys drown.
A nation dies like martyrs on a hill;
The dragon has become the daffodil.

Which is not very different from the sentiment expressed in a bard's fourteenth century *cywydd* about a town which had become thoroughly English:

*Lle bu'r Brython Saeson sydd,*
*A'r boen ar Gymru beunydd.*

(Where Britons dwelt now Saxons rule,
And Wales her loss each day shall mourn.)

The poet who wrote that would smile a certain smile today at this advertisement in the Liverpool *Daily Post*: 'Welsh property: well-built detached modern bungalow, Vale of Clwyd, beautiful surroundings, mostly Merseyside neighbours.'

Through their devotion to the Welsh language the people have kept a hold on their sense of nationhood. The language in their view is their differentia among the nations, a kind of identity disc, a thread connecting them with twenty centuries of history. To them the language *is* Wales. Today it is certainly a flag of idealism. And it is because the language is slipping into

20

quicksand, and those who care for it are aware of the pressures, that the language is a significant and central issue.

It is an issue that has produced a fine tension, for there can be no doubt that the relationship between the Welsh speakers and the people who do not have the language is increasingly important and will be crucial.

Three-quarters of the people of Wales do not speak Welsh and some of them regard the efforts being made to underpin the language as artificial and a waste of time and, more important, money. 'If everyone speaks English what's the point . . .?' There is a feeling, too, that the grip on the old language has held Wales back from complete unity with England, whatever that might mean, and that instead of being a unifying agent within Wales, it has divided.

The people agitating for the language are regarded by many other Welsh people simply as extremists and fanatics. Some become angry when efforts are made to introduce more Welsh into the schools. 'Filling up our children with that nonsense . . . they'd be better off teaching them French and German.'

The language exasperates because some Welsh people cannot grasp its fundamental importance to other Welsh people. It exasperates, too, simply because it cannot be understood: the moment the old language is spoken in the presence of English speakers there will be one or two who will bridle and complain afterwards about the rudeness of the Welsh speakers. There still exists a strong feeling, a carry-over from the days of repression of the language, that Welsh is rather second-rate.

Some English speakers get furious because they suspect that Welsh speakers regard themselves as better Welshmen for having the language. (Well, some Welsh speakers *do* regard themselves as better.) I wish I had a shilling for every time I have heard English-speaking Welshmen say, 'I'm just as good a Welshman as the Welsh speakers' and 'I'm all for promoting Welsh culture but . . .'. There is a suspicion that Welsh speakers operate a kind of mystic language freemasonry. People bridle when they see 'Welsh essential' on some job advertisements. Other people, of course, bridle when they note that the qualification is missing.

Welsh speakers complain bitterly that there is not enough

radio and television in their native tongue—the seven hours of Welsh language television every week produced by the BBC is derisory in their view. English speakers complain when Welsh programmes appear on their screens. The campaigns of the Welsh Language Society, a group largely of young people, who have daubed and uprooted road signs to draw attention to the status and plight of Welsh, causes quiet satisfaction in some quarters, fury in others: 'Why should a bloody minority impose its wishes on the majority?'

In a radio interview, Mr George Thomas, Secretary of State for Wales in the Labour Government, said that too much pressure from the Welsh language activists would produce a backlash from the English-speaking majority and cause the rise of 'an English language Paisley'. Emotive stuff, but the language issue in Wales is as emotional and fundamental and difficult to rationalize as love and hate.

The struggle for the language is not only an effort to safeguard a method of communication and a culture. It is part of the activity, which manifests itself all over the world in various forms, against the tendency of modern government, bureaucracy, technology, politics, big business and entertainment, to produce a crushing uniformity. Many young Welsh-speaking people who, in other situations elsewhere, might express their concern, anger and disenchantment at the state of the world through the underground press, by dropping out in one form or another, or by involving themselves in the relatively familiar streams of protest, turn their attention to the pressing situation on their own doorstep. They do not, however, reject patriotism, community and family. It is precisely these values, in a Welsh context, that they want to maintain.

It is often difficult to get people to talk reasonably about the language question. It seems that the English and Welsh languages are not simply heard, spoken or taught, they are invariably 'rammed down' people's throats. The matter is a hothouse in which thrive all manner of phobias, prejudices, inferiority complexes, half truths and unreasonableness. Rather like sex. As a Welshman smoothly assured me: 'There is absolutely no emotion over the language question. It is something got up by a few hooligans and intellectuals in North Wales and kept going by stupid newspapermen. It really makes me boil.' And he launched into a tirade.

To some extent he was concerned that the conflict over the language, with its manifestations of protest and publicity, was giving Wales a bad name over the border. It is a part of Welsh vulnerability, part of the conquered-country feeling, to worry about what the neighbour—England—thinks. The 'What-on-earth-will-they-think-of-us' letter is a common enough feature in newspapers after a Welsh demonstration has been reported in the national press and on television. It was particularly strongly revealed before the investiture of the Prince of Wales at Caernarvon in 1969 when there were many demonstrations against the event.

There is certainly a deal of bad feeling about the language, but there is a substantial body of goodwill, too, from the monoglot English Welshmen. The Anglo-Welshmen, very Welsh in his spirit and loyalty and instinct, but unable to speak or write in Welsh, is an important part of the modern literature scene in Wales.

It is curious that at a time when there are numerous black predictions about the future of Welsh, the language has the kind of vigour it has not had before.

For all their gloomy analyses, and the Welsh are given to self-examination of the pessimistic kind, history shows that, like their character, their culture has a granite core. Even granite can be eroded, of course, but Welsh language and culture have survived countless unhappy forecasts. And the people have a number of ancient prophecies to fall back on for comfort, like this one:

> Their Lord they will praise,
> Their speech they will keep,
> Their land they shall lose,
> Except wild Wales.

The struggle to secure the language is part of the new breeze in Wales in the 1970s. Along with a growing awareness of the past there is a shifting away from defeatism and a growth of confidence that Welsh people, as a nation, have not known for many years. It is far stronger than the boost that Lloyd George gave to Welsh pride. The old diffidence, even embarrassment, that people used to feel about being Welsh is vanishing.

The Welshman had an unflattering image in music-hall, fiction and popular belief. He was cloth-cap Taffy with coal-rimmed eyes, punctuating his yokel speech with 'indeed to goodness' and 'lookyou'—expressions that I have never heard Welsh people use. The Welshman was seen as thick, anti-drink, anti-joy. ('Can my wife and I have union on a Sunday, pastor?'—'Yes, providing you don't enjoy it.')

The old-fashioned belief about Wales persists. After all, people like to see their Irishmen portrayed as fighting drinkers shouting 'Begorrah' and their cowboys portrayed as knights of the saddle when, in fact, many of them were violent, ignorant and depraved. Recently, I saw South Wales depicted in a television play: the hero did the usual home-where-I-was-born cliché in a steep, terraced street, with a pit-wheel in the background, and then addressed The Welsh People, a group of slow-speaking, apparently thick-witted, cloth-capped diddymen who had yet to step into the twentieth century. Every group of people has its image of other groups, and the Welsh have their own caricature of Englishmen. The trouble until relatively recently has been that the easy-going Welshman came to believe the outsiders' image of himself. But all that is being gradually pushed out. The new feeling is Welsh-and-proud-of-it.

In the writings of Gerald the Welshman there is recorded the reply that an old man, at Pencader in Carmarthenshire, gave to Henry II when the king was campaigning and was seeking advice about the strength of the Welsh. The old man's statement is today preserved in granite at Pencader because it is a source of inspiration:

'This nation, O King, may often be weakened and in great part destroyed by the power of yourself and of others, but many a time, as it deserves, it will rise triumphant. But never will it be destroyed by the wrath of man, unless the wrath of God be added. Nor do I think that any other nation than this Wales, or any other tongue, whatever may hereafter come to pass, shall on the day of the great reckoning before the Most High Judge, answer for this corner of the earth.'

Today many of the people of this corner of the earth are concerned to keep the prophecy valid. The recognition of the fact that the culture is a threatened one is polarizing views and replacing apathy with determination. If it causes annoyance, argument, controversy and some strife, it cannot be, necessarily, a bad thing. I see no sign that the growth of the sense of identity and the mood of concern and willingness to do something about it will tail off, or even level off. The struggle to keep the traditional values is intensifying and is a very important part of the life and fibre of Wales today.

Long gone are the days when the *Encyclopaedia Britannica* could print, with arrogant and imperial cheek: *For Wales, see England.*

# 2 Perpetual incognito

In the elderly joke an Englishman in Wales sees a factory called Jones Manufacturing Company and muses: 'So that's where they make them.'

In Llanfyllin, one of the small towns of Montgomeryshire, there was a time when so many of the inhabitants bore the name of Jones that, on one occasion, Mr Jones, the magistrate, sentencing Jones the lawbreaker, who had been arrested by Constable Jones, said with a heavy humour: 'At least there will be one Jones less in Llanfyllin for twenty-one days.'

At the end of the last century it was seriously suggested that the government should establish a change-of-name registry in Wales so that the countless Joneses could be issued with new surnames and thus allow the machinery of bureaucracy to run more easily. Would Jones and his son and neighbour and cousin and friend have tramped from the valleys to a Department of Nomenclature, there to discard the most-used, the quintessential, Welsh surname, and emerge as Blacks, Browns, Whites, Blenkinsops and Delacourts? Some would. Some would have liked to adopt a distinctive and English-sounding title; they would have welcomed a chance to scrape off a bit of the Welshness. But I think most of the Joneses would have clung to the surname which is part of the tradition and the social history of their country. In the event, the colonial idea of a name registry came to nothing and the head-counters gritted their teeth and scratched on through the endless lists of Joneses.

There is a resigned sigh between the lines of the Registrar-General's report of 1853: 'The name of John Jones is in Wales a perpetual incognito.' A report of a court case in Caernarvonshire in 1894, in which most of the witnesses shared the same surname, talks despairingly of the proceedings being 'a patronymical Bedlam' and adds: 'This action was certainly an object lesson in nomenclature to all Welshmen.' The Welsh Press emphasized the desirability of a thorough change in Welsh surnames.

The Welsh people themselves answered the need for identification with the nickname. Jones the Bread, the Milk, the Post, Flatnose Jones and Jones King's Arms have been a part of life in the valleys for well over a century. And although they live on still in the small and close communities they are fading away, like the community spirit of the old days in which they throve. Few people under the age of forty keep up the custom of nicknames. The names are a part of the music-hall image of Wales and have been a piquant part of its history. But by the end of the century they will have all but vanished.

In a land where there is a paucity of surnames the nicknames have fulfilled the important social purpose of identification as well as appealing to the Welshman's sense of comedy. In most communities any physical quirk, any deviation from the norm, a limp or big ears, a wart or big feet, a stammer or a big ego, a fondness for a particular dish or constant use of one word, was the target for a nickname.

Poor Harry Greensuit and Jones Spats. They bore these names for decades after the youthful sartorial follies which earned them the labels. Dai Quiet Wedding was poor and got married in plimsolls. Dai Death Club was the man from the insurance company. Dai Piano was so called, not for his keyboard ability, but for cadging cigarettes. As he helped himself from the packets of his long-suffering friends, they would ask: 'No cigarettes today, Dai?'—'No, left them home on the piano.'

Jones Balloon was a foreman who once implored his men: 'Don't let me down, boys.' Mrs Dai Eggs was married to an egg seller in Swansea. From the day she gave birth to twins she was Mrs Dai Double-yolk. A man who constantly prefaced his sentences with 'I'll tell you what will happen, boys . . .' was known as Glyn Prediction.

Emlyn Kremlin was a Communist. A man with a limp was Dai Up-and-Down. The man at the Llanelli rugby ground who always called to the rushing forwards in a voice of thunder: 'Feet! Feet!' was eternally Dai Foot-and-Mouth. Sid Loud Hailer was a miner of stentorian tone. Sir David Maxwell Fyfe, a Minister for Welsh Affairs, was known from Cardiff to Caernarvon as Dai Bananas. A Mr Harse was called Dai Bum. A Mr Thomas Thomas was Tom Twice.

WALES AND THE WELSH

Most of the people of Wales share a few surnames. The most common are Jones, Davies, Thomas, Hughes, Roberts, Evans, Griffiths, Lewis and Williams. Surnames in Wales did not develop as they did in England. English surnames evolved in the Middle Ages as the populations of towns began to grow and the administrators and the people themselves demanded identification. The names were usually formed from trades, physical characteristics, colour of clothing or the site of a man's home or work.

In Wales, however, there were few native surnames. The most common were Gwynn or Winn, from the word meaning white, Lloyd, from *llwyd* meaning grey, Vaughan from *fychan*, meaning little. Most of the people maintained the ancient tradition of the patronymic, for love of genealogy is a Welsh characteristic— 'They esteem noble birth and generous descent above all things', wrote Gerald the Welshman in the twelfth century. In any case a pedigree was a man's title deed through which he claimed his birthright. Men took their fathers' first names as surnames and usually added their grandfathers' and great-grandfathers' names, too, often going back six or seven generations. They used the word ap or ab, meaning son of, and the equivalent to Mac in Scotland and O in Ireland, to connect the names. Thus, in the small rural communities of Wales, when a man was announced as Huw ap Robert ap Ifan ap Guto ap Huw, everyone knew exactly who he was.

Anglesey's Member of Parliament in 1541 was Richard ap David ap Hugh Ieuan ap Geffrey. And the bailiff of Llan-fyllin in 1585 styled himself as Cadwaladr ap David ap John ap Hugh ap Moris. These Welsh names were a source of merriment in England and one mediaeval wag wrote that cheese would have to be re-defined as 'ap curds ap milk ap cow ap grass ap earth.' The oldest English joke about the patronymic of Wales concerns an Englishman riding home one dark night. He heard a cry from a ravine and stopped. 'Who's there?' he called. 'Sion ap Ifan ap Robert ap Ieuan ap Huw ap Huw,' was the answer. 'Lazy fellows that ye be,' cried the Englishman, spurring horse, 'to lie rolling in that hole, half a dozen of ye—why in the name of commonsense don't ye help one another out!'

28

The spread of church and state administration in the reign of Henry VIII, particularly after the Act of Union of 1536, was an important factor in the adoption of settled surnames. The Act stipulated that English should be the language of administration and the Welsh gentry began to desert the customs and the language of Wales and copy English ways. The king himself, although of Welsh extraction, was said to have had an aversion to the patronymics of Wales and commanded his ministers to oppose the custom. For this reason Thomas ap Richard ap Howell ap Ieuan of Mostyn appeared before the Lord President of Wales and was ordered to take Mostyn as his surname, to content himself 'with one name—like a Christian'. He did.

In the thinly populated mountain areas of Wales surnames were not necessary, but settled surnames began to develop on English lines in the border areas of Monmouthshire, Radnorshire and Flintshire in the sixteenth century.

Welshmen seeking a fixed surname usually clung to the patronymic tradition and chose their fathers' first name. They anglicized it, or had it anglicized for them by the clerks of church, court and government. So that Ifan ap Ifan became Evan Evans, or Evan Bevan; and Sion ap Sion (Sion is one of the Welsh forms of John and pronounced Shon) became John Johns, or John Jones. As John in its various forms—Iwan, Ieuan, Ifan, Ioan—was the most popular Welsh Christian name it was inevitable that Jones should become the most-used surname.

The English clerks who had to grapple with the strange Welsh names often wrote down a name that only roughly matched the spoken native form. One can imagine the grumbling ledger-keepers scratching away at their lists . . .

'Name?'

'Sion ap Dafydd.' The quill squeaking it down as John Davies.

'Next.'

'Tomos ap Hywel.' Into the book as Thomas Powell.

Thus Iwan ap Huw became John Hughes, or Pugh; Llwyd became Lloyd or Floyd or Flood; Llewelyn became Fluellin, or Wellings; Maredudd became Merrydew or Meredith; Gruffydd became Griffiths; ap Rhys became Rice or Price; Guto became

29

Gittings. There are about 450 of these anglicized Welsh names but fewer than fifty are in popular use.

The story of the English bureaucracy's struggle with the tongue-knotting names of Wales was put into this nineteenth century comic verse about a judge sorting out a crowd of people in his court:

> Then strove the judge with main and might
> The sounding consonants to write.
> But when the day was almost gone
> He found his work not nearly done,
> His ears assailed most woefully
> With names like Rhys ap Griffith Ddu,
> Aneirin, Iorwerth, Ieuan Goch,
> And Llywarch Hen o Abersoch,
> Taliesin ap Llewelyn Fawr
> And Llun ap Arthur bach y Cawr.
> Until at length, in sheer despair,
> He doffed his wig and tore his hair
> And said he would no longer stand
> The surnames of our native land.
> Take ten, he said, and call them Rice;
> Take other ten and call them Price;
> Take fifty others call them Pughs,
> A hundred more I'll dub them Hughes;
> Now Roberts name some hundred score
> And Williams name a legion more.
> And call, he moaned in languid tone,
> Call all the other thousands—Jones.

The *Lays of Modern Oxford* says this about Jesus College, which has a strong Welsh tradition:

> From Jesus in whose ancient quad
> If stranger thou hast ever trod,
> And yelled the name of Jones—
> From east and west, and south and north
> A score of anxious heads pop forth
> All Welshmen, each of whom can claim
> That ancient and time-honoured name.

Until relatively recently some Welshmen still had no settled surname. In a case heard in the London law courts in 1891 a man from Caernarvonshire could not provide a definite name: he was Henry Evans and Henry Thomas and Henry Thomas Evans. The patronymic with the connecting ap has survived to this day. The founder of the Welsh youth movement *Urdd Gobaith Cymru* was Sir Ifan ab Owen Edwards; and a number of Welshmen still like to maintain the ancient name-form.

By the time that the epoch of ruthless mining was under way in South Wales the Joneses and Evanses and Davies and Williamses were legion. As the people moved into the crowded, smudged and blackened valleys the need for identification became vital.

To create a little distinction some people, particularly those who had, or felt they had, some authority or standing, added their mothers' maiden names to their surnames: Parry-Jones, Vaughan-Thomas, Lloyd-Evans, Parry-Williams. Ministers of religion often added a middle name: the Rev. John Elfyn Jones, for example. Some people took place names for distinction. A Welsh barrister who moved to Sydenham in Kent avoided confusion by styling himself Mr Sydenham Jones.

In most communities a man's occupation has always been a good way of identifying him. Dai Bread, Phil Butcher, Tom the Post, Jones the Meat, have been familiar in Wales for generations.

In many towns the Co-operative shop manager has been known as Jones y Cop. A photographer in Carmarthenshire was Eddie Click Click. Jones the Stitch was a tailor. And the man who rolled a barrel of ale to the foundry for the thirsty metal workers was known as Will *Casgen-gwrw*—Will Beerbarrel.

Strangers to a district were often given the name of the town or area they came from: Georgie Bargoed, Tommy Bala, Shoni Aberdare, for example. *Sais* is the Welsh word for Englishman and many who have settled in Wales have been known as John *y Sais*.

People who kept, or were born in, public houses were often given the pub's name: Jones King's Arms, for instance. Farmers took—still take—the names of their farms: Jones *Craig-ddu*. Coalminers were often called after the pits they worked in: Evans Deep Duffryn, Jones Great Western and Williams Navigation. Or even after the seam they usually laboured in: Two-foot Jones was a man who worked in the confines of the two-foot seam.

In the nineteenth and twentieth centuries the growth of the chapel movement led to a fashion for Biblical names. Many parents gladdened the minister's heart, and piously brightened Jones, with Isaac, Mordecai, Shadrack, Hezekiah, Joshua and Moses. Obadiah Evans and Methuselah Jones, for instance, were well-known miners' leaders. Some of the Biblical names became surnames when men were deciding on a settled name. Thus Morgan the son of Joshua Jones became Morgan Joshua and transmitted the surname to his descendants. There was a fashion at one time for the 'double-Biblical'—Moses Moses, Enoch Enoch and so on. Composers' names enjoyed a wave of popularity, particularly in the first twenty years of this century, and many a baby left his baptism ceremony as Verdi Jones or Handel Hughes.

The nicknames of Wales not only sorted out the Joneses. They were a game, too, and newcomers to a community and young men as yet un-nicknamed, were eyed up for the idio- syncrasy, or the fatal step outside the accepted norm or the habit that could be nailed with a name. A friend told me about an Evans who moved into a valley village and was warned to be careful because some of the villagers had a cruel wit when it came to nicknames. 'Don't worry about me,' Evans said, 'I'm too clever to be caught like that.' He never fathomed why his neighbours referred to him as Clever Evans.

A tight-fisted Carmarthenshire man was known as Owen One-I-Got because whenever he was asked for a sweet or cigar- ette he invariably had just one left in the packet. 'Only one I got,' he would say, putting the bag or packet away.

In one of the valleys of Monmouthshire Amen Jones and Jones Hallelujah were devout men whose ringing responses in the chapel, intended to attract the attention of the Almighty, succeeded only in grating in the ears of the rest of the congrega- tion.

Exactly Jones was named after his favourite word; Jones Caerphilly always had cheese sandwiches for his lunch and Dai

Brown Ale drank nothing else. Jones Popbottle drank nothing
alcoholic for he was a well-known teetotaller in his valley town.
In his pursuit of temperance he was simply following the lead
of St David himself, who drank only water, and was known as
Dewi *Ddyfrwr*—David the water drinker. Mrs Thomas Pay
Cash abhorred hire purchase, but Billy Never-Never was a
celibate.

Places, as well as people, have been given nicknames. The
Anglo-Celtic Watch Company at Ystradgynlais is still known to
Welsh people as *Ffatri Tic-Toc*. The national *eisteddfod* of 1917,
when the prize of the bardic chair was awarded to a poet who
had been killed in action, is still known as the *Eisteddfod* of the
Black Chair.

There was a time in many communities when no one slipped
through the nickname net. A man who went to a quarry for a
job answered 'Dai Jones' when the foreman asked for his name.
'Jones, eh,' the foreman said thoughtfully. 'We've six Joneses
here already, man. You'll have to have a nickname.' And he
began to run an eye over him, perhaps in search of a squint, a
six-fingered hand or oversize feet. Fearing the worst, Jones said
with a stiff dignity: 'Well, if you have to give me a bloody name,
give me something substantial.'

He was known for ever as Dai Substantial.

# 3 'We are a musical nation'

I mentioned to an English friend that I was going to the Royal National *Eisteddfod* of Wales.

'Off to the Ku-Klux-Klan, eh?' he said with a grin.

When I got there, a grave man, with hands bent from pulpit-gripping and forehead furrowed from an excess of complex alliterative verse, intoned: 'The *eisteddfod* is the apex of the cultural life of our nation.'

'The *eisteddfod*,' said another man, not so grave, 'is the occasion when a lot of Welsh people have a very happy time and there is a great feeling of love and patriotism and a few pretty girls, on a purely temporary basis, you understand, relinquish a little of their virginity.'

The trouble with explaining the phenomenon of the *eisteddfod* and its irresistible fascination for the Welsh-speaking community is that it is not just something you can attend and relate afterwards as a series of facts. It is an atmosphere. A free-fall parachutist, after all, can never communicate completely the attraction and sensation of his sport to a non-participant. He can say that he jumped, and, later, landed. But you have to jump with him to understand exactly what he's getting at. And you have to be an *eisteddfodwr* to understand the *eisteddfod* and to derive the full benefit of the treatment.

In modern terms it is a happening, admittedly an engineered one, but with a basic framework for happy spontaneity. There is a cultural focus, but what goes on, on the stage, is not necessarily the most important part of it. What is also important is simply to be there, splashing about in the people-bath, to have a common interest and to enjoy an intimate communal experience. The *eisteddfod* is, in essence, a tribal gathering, an enormous Celtic picnic, a time to meet old friends, shake hands, talk Welsh shop, join societies, bury hatchets, hatch plots, sing songs and—off the *eisteddfod* field—talk for hours and drink beer.

To the uninitiated the spectacle of the ceremonial aspects of the *eisteddfod*, the ritual with the great sword, the horn, the crown, the proclamations, the dancing elves, arouses a smile or a snigger and it is easy to dismiss the whole business as a strange manifestation of a dying culture, or the playtime of 'that lot in Druid Land'. The ceremonial side of the *eisteddfod* is the facet most often presented outside Wales on television and in the newspapers.

Not everyone approves of the druidic ritual. After the 1971 *eisteddfod* a Church of England clergyman was fined £20 for telephoning a fake warning that a bomb had been lodged under the main pavilion. He admitted he had been the author of a letter to the local paper describing the *eisteddfod* and the *gorsedd* of bards as 'a pagan institution'.

I must confess that it is difficult to keep a straight face when the two ceremonial trumpeters, like large red pixies advancing on a Welsh Jericho, blow those cracked fanfares. The dressing up is a target for ribald comment but, although the *eisteddfodwyr* take the ceremonial with a measure of seriousness, they do not make the mistake of taking it too seriously.

The be-nightied bards and the harp-accompanied ceremonies may look amusing to English eyes, but there is in most ceremonial an element of the ludicrous. It exists in the dressing-up rituals in state, military, municipal and religious contexts everywhere. And, in terms of mere sartorial amusement, there is not much difference between the head-dress and robes of an archdruid and the false hair and swaddling-robes of a British judge.

As an essentially Welsh language festival the *eisteddfod* is regarded in Wales as either very important or very unimportant.

In his column in the *South Wales Echo*, Herbert Williams expressed what many of the people of Wales, particularly southeast Wales, feel about the national *eisteddfod*. 'If people want to sing, dance, become crowned bards and dress up in nightshirts, why not?' he wrote.

'It's just that it means so much to some people and so little to others. In my particular neck of the woods, it falls far short of Come Dancing and the International Horse Show in terms of appeal. . . . There's a great deal to laugh at in the *eisteddfod*. The

35

*gorsedd* robes are outrageously funny, and how these people can bring themselves to wear them is beyond me. There is also a great deal of pomposity, and a snivelling pride in being bilingual and thus on the side of the angels. But there's a lot to admire, if only grudgingly. It's something, after all, for hundreds of people to spend months of their time writing vast chunks of poetry or prose. . . . It's something, too, for football-size crowds to come together for a cultural festival.

'But I can't bring myself to go there. It's not my scene at all. I doubt if I'd go there even if I spoke the blasted language. It's such an in-thing, isn't it? It's so cosy, so disgustingly uplifting. There isn't even a beer tent, and that, dear friends, is chapel morality at its worst.'

There is no genuine equivalent to the *eisteddfod* in England. There just isn't the same need. The *eisteddfod* exists and succeeds because it is a celebration of the Welsh language and a gathering for a distinct minority. The aim of the *eisteddfod*, according to its constitution, is to sustain Welsh culture and to safeguard the Welsh language. But, as I have indicated, what happens on the stage is not the only thing the people go for, and you do not, in my experience, need to speak Welsh, to derive a good deal of pleasure from it.

Many Welshmen, it seems, need to recharge their spiritual batteries every now and then. By the end of a year they are just about ready for the exhilarating experience of the *eisteddfod* and the reaffirmation of identity that goes with it. By the end of the great week—and many thousands take their holidays to coincide with it—tens of thousands of Welsh men and women emerge glowing, refreshed and cleansed from total immersion in their cultural Ganges, a steady warming at the fire of their Welshness and an unselfconscious celebration of themselves. 'You come away with the feeling of exhilaration that you get after hearing a damn good sermon,' an *eisteddfodwr* said. 'Your soul has been bared and your hair has been let down.'

One of the leading figures of Welsh cultural life, the late Sir Albert Evans-Jones, wrote: 'Doubtless one of the attractions that draws them together is the natural desire for an annual reunion with old friends; but a still deeper attraction lies in their love of Wales, its ancient tongue and its traditional culture,

36

and their demand for fellowship with others who love the same things. This is a love that calls Welshmen home to their *eisteddfod* even from the ends of the earth. If the *eisteddfod* is to be held in your district, remember that you are receiving a very special privilege. . . . To your town, as pilgrims to a shrine, Welshmen will stream from afar. . . .'

The great pavilion, seating 9000 people, is the focus of the week. The culture bit of the *eisteddfod*, the competitions for dancers, singers, poets, harpers, reciters, choirs and the rest, takes place in here. The Scots toss cabers when they meet; the less hairy Welsh compete with singing and cunning verses. Most people have an interest in some of the events, and there are times when the pavilion is packed and crowds have to stand outside and listen to the proceedings over the public address system. But there is a fair proportion of people who would not miss the *eisteddfod* for anything—yet never show their faces inside the pavilion.

'I've been coming here for twelve years,' a man said as he perambulated around the *eisteddfod* field, 'and I have never been in the pavilion.' He said it with a kind of pride, as if he had, every year, detected and skirted a minefield.

He was one of those who journey to the *eisteddfod* purely for its other great activity, meeting friends and talking. All around *y maes*—the field—you can see the arms go up in semaphored greeting as individuals and groups catch sight of each other, alter course and fire off a fusillade of greetings and smiles.

'Huw!'

'Emrys!'

'Sorry to hear about your mother.'

'The adjudicator is mad.'

'Our Rhiannon is in the choir.'

'A poem of pure gold.'

'Kicked it over from thirty yards.'

'In the family way.'

'The standard's gone right down this year, man.'

'You look twelve months older.'

'Out of the scrum and gone like a whippet.'

'Called me a bloody nationalist.'

'Have you met Miss Jones?'

D

The little molecules of the newly-met pump hands, slap backs and talk all at once. The heads are bent in eager gossip and laughter; there are spasms of laughter from the knots of people bent over copies of *Lol*, a scurrilous magazine of wit, lampoons and nudes, brought out for every *eisteddfod*, and certainly not for the manse market. Around the small tents and pavilions of myriad small societies are the informal discussion groups and impromptu teach-ins where the talk is of politics, nationalism, the language and the Welsh condition. Wales is the most-discussed subject and all the talking is done to a background of harp music and singing relayed from the pavilion. The groups disintegrate, then rapidly reform with different individuals but with much the same roundabout of conversation. The *eisteddfod* field is a kind of Welsh Piccadilly. The Welsh-speaking world goes round and round and a man might easily meet every one of his friends and acquaintances here. 'And, let's face it, you keep in touch with the people you don't want to meet more than once a year,' an *eisteddfodwr* said, lest I should get the idea that mutual admiration was boundless.

Away from the *eisteddfod* field, in the nearest public houses, there occur the smaller unofficial and alcoholic *eisteddfodau*. Here there is more singing and hard talking and the standard of drinking in some cases is, to say the least, vigorous. Those licensees and hoteliers who remove the antiques and valuables from their bars prior to *eisteddfod* week have no wish to doubt the integrity of the average *eisteddfodwr*, but it is best that decks are cleared for action and, in any case, the first week of August just happens to be a convenient time to take down the brasses and copper and glassware for cleaning.

Sometimes people grumble that the *eisteddfod* itself is dry, in keeping with the Welsh tradition. 'Chapel morality at its worst.' They point to the fact that leading cultural figures plainly enjoy a social pint and see in this a hypocrisy. But by my observation it is no bad thing that the dedicated *eisteddfodwyr* who feature in the evening revels have a day of milk shakes and tea beforehand and, by the look of them, a day of milk shakes and tea afterwards.

Although no beer tent is ever erected on the *eisteddfod* field, there are minute drops of liquor to be found in quiet corners

38

and the word spreads quickly. Sometimes one or two of the business concerns who have a pavilion on the field provide a bottle of bootleg sherry for special guests and customers, but whenever I have tracked it down it has all gone. The heliographic glint of a hip flask in the midday sunshine betrays the guilty and the weak-willed, but in the main, those who would normally compare brands of bitter and mild beer at this time are to be found comparing the rival qualities of strawberry and banana milk shakes, and telling themselves how much better they feel for it.

As a great meeting place and cultural festival, the *eisteddfod* is one of the natural and necessary institutions of Welsh life. It was founded in its present form in the last century and was one of the aims in the movement for institutions that went with the burgeoning of national self-awareness in Wales. The University of Wales, the national library, the national museum and the *eisteddfod* became important projects at a time when Wales was reawakening, wanting to assert its own character and nationhood and preserve its special qualities. It was an extension of the same feeling that later led to the move for a capital of Wales.

There have been *eisteddfodau*, or meetings of bards, in Wales for more than a thousand years. The *gorsedd*, or circle, of bards and the ritual that goes with it is pseudo-druidic. It was invented at the end of the eighteenth century by a gifted poet called Iolo Morgannwg. The *gorsedd* was intended at first to be an exclusive guild of poets but it eventually became a part of the *eisteddfod* and, although criticized as phoney, satisfies the need felt by most communities for some harmless ritual. The event held at Llangollen in 1858 is regarded as something of a starting point for the modern *eisteddfod* but it was, by all accounts, an odd affair. Some of the competitions were fixed and the organizers made a large profit. There were a number of strange, and what would now be termed hippy, characters in the leading roles including Dr William Price of Llantrisant, wearing a fox-skin hat and a sword.

The national *eisteddfod* was put on a firm footing in 1880, with the setting up of the National *Eisteddfod* Association, now reshaped as the Court of the National *Eisteddfod*. Traditionally, the *eisteddfod* is held alternately in North and South Wales and the pavilion and its ancillary buildings are moved from one site to the next like a vast Welsh Big Top. The *gorsedd* of bards which shares the administration of the festival, is the repository of ritual and its tripod symbol represents God and the divine attributes of love, justice and truth. At every town or village where an *eisteddfod* is held a circle of *gorsedd* stones is erected. The *eisteddfod* rites take place within the circle and the stones are left, so that these necklets of rock, puzzling to visitors, are all over Wales.

All the *gorsedd* ceremonies are accompanied by the harp and sessions begin when the six-foot long grand sword—*y cleddyf mawr*—is partly withdrawn from its sheath. It is never withdrawn entirely because it is a symbolic sword of peace, always carried by its point and 'never held, borne or bared against any human being'.

As the sword is partly withdrawn from the scabbard the archdruid makes the ritual challenge:

'*A oes heddwch?*'—'Is it peace?'

And the assembled people shout back at him:

'*Heddwch!*'—'Peace!'

Other parts of the ritual are the offering of a horn, symbolizing a gift of wine, and the *aberthged*, a sheaf of corn; and then a group of girls with flowers in their hair dance barefoot.

Watching all of this are the bards in their thin gowns and hoods. Those in green are of the ovate order and have either passed two *gorsedd* examinations or have been honoured for services to Welsh culture. The blue bards are of the order of bards, musicians and literati, and have passed the final examination. Those in white are of the druidic order to which they have been admitted in recognition of a substantial contribution to the culture of Wales.

Members of the *gorsedd* often take a formal bardic name, derived from a place or landmark or early Welsh literature, and sometimes they become well known by it. Elfed, Crwys, Gwylfa were famous bardic names in the past. And, recently, on the death of Sir Albert Evans-Jones, distinguished poet and *eisteddfod* figure, universally known by his bardic name of

Cynan, the message on the newspaper posters throughout Wales was, perfectly adequately, 'Cynan dies'.

The two major bardic competitions at the national *eisteddfod* are for the chair and for the crown. The chair is a wooden throne, often quite handsome, and the winner takes it away with him and it becomes a prized piece of furniture in his home. The bardic chair can only be won for an *awdl*, a composition written in strict metres of a traditional form of verse. It is difficult stuff to write. The crown is awarded for a *pryddest*, which is poetry in free metres.

The announcement of the winners of chair and crown is always a suspenseful affair, with a well-organized spontaneity. The pavilion is packed and the *gorsedd* assembles on the stage. The winning bard's name is read out and a spotlight bathes him in brightness as he rises shyly from his seat in the crowd. The identity of the winner is a secret until his name is called and, although he himself has received the official whisper, he is expected to adopt a modest 'Who? Me?' expression as the spotlight seeks him out.

One of the important ingredients of the *eisteddfod* is keen competition. Proud parents, white-knuckled, and keen coaches, tight-lipped, are in the background as the competitors go on stage and the excitement is like that at any sporting event. On the field one day I saw a group of girls huddled around a loud-speaker which was relaying the results of their competition. Some of them were weeping because they had lost and the others were weeping because they had won.

The competitive aspect of the festival is ideal for featuring on television. During the 1971 national *eisteddfod* at Bangor, BBC Wales got down to basics and opted out of the national network, much to the annoyance of some of the BBC hierarchy in London, to put on its own Welsh 'Grandstand' of Saturday afternoon sporting events. There was Rugby football and, from the *eisteddfod*, a male voice choir competition. Such a combination must have left many Welsh viewers blinking through a haze of patriotic feeling.

The great choirs, their voices thundering down the valleys from Caernarvon to Cardiff, are a part of the land-of-song image that Wales presents to the world, part of the welcome in

41

the hillside. But in the past twenty years or so the choral tradition has been in decline. It is not that Wales is losing its voice; it is simply that it is gaining a more varied and sophisticated one and the major choral competitions of the national *eisteddfod* are no longer relevant to the big choirs and other choral groups which have been developing in Wales.

There is a certain pride taken in the old label 'land of song', and although Wales is no more or less musical than many other countries, a large number of Welsh people are fairly easily moved to a burst of song. Welsh pub singing on my observation is about as awful as English pub singing, but where Englishmen require a pint or two to release inhibitions and activate the vocal chords, Welshmen will get going without the catalyst.

Once, on the *eisteddfod* field, I saw a man go to a music firm's stand and try a few bars on a small organ on display. His companion began to hum a hymn tune and the soft sound was heard by two passers-by who walked in to add a quiet tenor and soprano. Several men gossiping nearby broke off their conversation to put some bone into the tenor line, three housewives quickly finished their milkshakes and walked over to add their voices, and a brace of preachers, as bees to nectar, came in to make the whole business more or less official. By the seventh or eighth verse there were about sixty people singing strongly, there was some cunning harmonizing going on, and the man who, in the first place, had simply gone in to play a few notes on the organ, now had the *hwyl* and the holy sweat upon him and was playing with a fervent vigour as if his very soul was vibrating. This vigour and the crowd's enthusiasm, did not abate for a full hour.

The musical tradition of Wales was created largely by the chapels. Community singing did not need patronage and could be enjoyed by the poorest people. In bursts of fervour some congregations sang all day, or even went on for two days, with hymns stretching to twenty and thirty and more verses. There was a danger at one time that the older musical heritage of Wales would be swept away under the wave of nonconformist religion. The chapels frowned on the folk dances and the bright tunes. The native instruments, the *pibgorn*, a pipe, and the *crwth*, a stringed instrument, had disappeared by the beginning of the nineteenth century, and the Welsh harp only just survived to this century. Fortunately, a large number of native songs and melodies were written down, and thus saved, by collectors. The chapels could not, in any case, ignore all the folk songs and some of the traditional tunes became hymns.

The chapel choirs were firmly established by the middle of the nineteenth century. In the twenty-five years after 1850 choral music spread and developed by leaps and bounds. In this period new teaching methods, the mixed and male voice choirs and the *cymanfa ganu* (a festival of hymn singing), became an important part of the music and social life of Wales. The fame of Welsh choirs spread and the Welsh love of singing became part of the country's image. When the line '*Mor o gan yw Cymru i gyd*'—'All Wales is a sea of song'—was written, it reflected with little exaggeration the mood at the time.

The *eisteddfod* was caught up and swept along in the swelling tide of song. It had to change from being largely a literary and poetry event to accommodate the choir movement and it began to ring to the sounds of the massed voices. Throughout Wales the lights burned late in the chapels as the valleys resounded to the sound of the men at choir practice. The element of competition between choirs intensified and during the *eisteddfod* excitement and rivalry made the choral contests unforgettable occasions. During the weeks before the major competitions choirs tried to discover how the opposition was singing particular pieces and spies with well-turned ears were despatched to listen to the rival choirs in practice and report back.

The great age of mighty choral singing in Wales lasted from the 1860s to the Second World War, although it began to fade in the First World War. The loosening of the chapels' grip on Wales—and the growth of the entertainment industry—meant that chapel-based activities declined and the choirs as a movement gradually lost their former strength. But while Wales has lost much of the power of its old voice, it has gained a new one. There are new choirs, but these are not rooted in the chapels. They are smaller, modern and objective, experimental, favouring cosmopolitan music and works especially written for them. The *eisteddfod* is hardly relevant to them. A good deal of the spirit of the new choral expression is found in choirs like the

Cardiff Polyphonic and the Rhondda's Pendyrus, both setting new standards.

Many of the older generation find all this new singing a little baffling. And, fortunately for those who enjoy the sensation of hearing great choirs going about their business with the big works and the traditional hymns and songs, there is still, in spite of the decline, a surprising amount of the fine old-fashioned choral singing in Wales.

The sound of Welsh people working at their songs is something that people expect to hear in Wales. Singing is so strongly associated with Wales that Welshmen are almost expected to have a sweet and natural vocal ability. As a kind of birthright.

The souvenir manufacturers, as you would expect, know the importance of cliché. The tea towels made in England, the ash-trays made in Birmingham, and the postcards made in Spain, carry the message, 'Wales—Land of Song'.

The phrase was valid enough in the golden years of the choirs and today there is still an appreciation of good choral singing, and an awareness of the tradition, that provides an element of truth to what is a heavily overworked generalization.

Maybe Dylan Thomas had his tongue in his cheek when he made his *Under Milk Wood* minister, the Rev. Eli Jenkins, exclaim: 'Praise the Lord! We are a musical nation.' Some critics sniff at the idea that Wales is a musical nation and point to the gaps in its musical development. There have been, and still are, weaknesses, but the critics have often failed to look at the background.

Wales has traditionally been a nation of amateur singers, actors and artists. Its art has largely been community art and developed without patronage. Voices are cheaper than instruments, so that the instrumental side in Welsh music developed more slowly than the choral side. Thus, when people scoff at the concept of Wales, the land of culture, and say with truth: 'Wales has no national theatre, no national orchestra, no concert hall in its capital, no opera house,' they are being unfair. Of course, the frustrations are enormous. It was frustration which made Sir Geraint Evans, in October 1971, threaten never to sing in Wales again unless the facilities for opera were greatly improved. 'It is second best all the time ... and I am fed up with seeing second best in Wales.' Lack of money is at the root of most of the trouble; the arts in Wales in the past ten or fifteen years have steadily become more professional, modern, sophisticated, and the revolution has not been paced by the creation of the necessary facilities. Wales has a rich and vigorous cultural life. Give it some time, and a lot of money, and it will sort out the anomalies and catch up with the pressing demands of its own cultural revolution.

The musical instrument associated with Wales is the one that those flinty preachers of long ago almost got rid of in the great drive against sin, the harp. The haunting sound of the harp has been a part of the folk culture of Wales for more than a thousand years and the instrument has been a sacred possession for Welshmen up and down the centuries. Indeed, in the twelfth century, old Welsh law decreed that any of a Welshman's possessions could be seized for debt, except his harp.

The harp, of course, is played from the heart and is in tune with the soul. In 1899 a Welsh bard gave this advice to harpers (a harper is a harp player, a harpist is a professional harper) in a letter: 'A pure Welsh Harper (one who has love for his country) ought to be well averst with the history of his country —and to be acquinted with the mountains, vallis, rocks, rivers, dingeles and dales—so as to be able to give a true sound to his national music he ought to have a smile on his face or a teer in his eye.'

Today there is a renewed and growing interest in harp playing, which means that John Thomas, the only professional harp maker in Wales, and one of only a handful in Britain, is much in demand. His waiting list is at least two-and-a-half years long. His workshop, called *Telynfa*—the place of the harp —is at Gwaelod-y-Garth, near Cardiff, and is filled with bits of harps and timber. He cannibalizes old furniture, Victorian wardrobes and sideboards, for their walnut and mahogany. He knows that some people like to have a harp as a status symbol, to keep on show in the best room, but, a craftsman to the marrow, he avoids making harps for people who want them just for decoration.

'I like to know that my harps are going to good homes where they will be played by folks who love them. I can tell at once

45

when people have a love of the harp. Not long ago a man of eighty or so brought his harp in for repair. I could tell he was very fond of it and I mended it right away. When he got it home he was so thrilled that he rang me up, put the telephone close to the harp strings and gave me a recital. To many Welsh people, you see, the harp is a sacred thing.

'I'm deeply devoted to it. It is the oldest musical instrument in the world. People were drawing sound from harps more than three thousand years ago. Like women and sailing ships they have beautiful curves and when you play the harp it is a very personal experience. You put your cheek against the neck, you embrace it, and when you touch the strings you create the oldest musical sound in the world. It is the music of heaven.

# 4 Not English'd out

The Lleyn peninsula is the hook of land in the north-west, with the drop of holy Bardsey Island at the end of its nose. It gropes out for Ireland and lies well beyond Snowdonia's wall and therefore stayed out of the reach of English influences longer than any other part of Wales. The thin, visiting Irish rain and a mist from the sea were masking Lleyn's beauty when I went to see Mrs Mary Roberts. She was ninety-four years old and had lived all her life a few miles from the village of Aberdaron, and seventy of them in the farmhouse where she now sat beside the kitchen range, pinafored, neat and alert, offering tea and cakes which her son served. I needed an interpreter to talk with Mrs Roberts because she is one of the handful of people who are the remnants of a Wales that has all but gone: the Welsh monoglots. She knew about half as many phrases in English as I knew in Welsh. 'Good day', 'bad day', and 'No speak English' were her limit.

The Education Act of 1870 brought English teaching to many parts of Wales, but, for a long time, education in some rural districts was patchy. In any case, the strength of the nonconformist faith, riveted to the Welsh language, was an important element of resistance to English, particularly in remote parts. There was sometimes the ludicrous situation of Englishmen trying to school classes of Welsh children who could not understand a word they were saying.

Mr Gruffudd Parry, a Lleyn schoolmaster and playwright, who interpreted Mrs Roberts's conversation for me, recalled that he knew no English when he went to the grammar school at Caernarvon at the age of twelve. His experience was typical of that of many Welsh people who are now in middle age. 'The schoolmasters were talking away in English and we couldn't understand them. But we learned very quickly, mainly from the other boys at first. Looking back, it seems that we became fluent English speakers almost overnight.'

47

In some schools in the last century teachers tried to pumice-stone the stain of Welsh by fining children or making those who spoke it wear a wooden board around their necks. This dunce-cap device was called the Welsh Not: it had the words Welsh Not or the initials W.N. inscribed upon it. At the start of the school day the first child caught speaking Welsh by the teacher was made to wear the board and the victim could only get rid of it when he heard a classmate speak in Welsh. At the end of the day the pupil wearing the board was caned. Today the mention of the Welsh Not brings a flash of anger to many people in Wales. It was crude and cruel, of course, but it was used in an age when such devices were considered suitable and its intention was considered by many as laudable: to help give a child the privilege and the window-on-the-world of English. It was a time, after all, when some noted patriot writers and poets wrote their letters and kept their diaries in English and went to English chapels rather than Welsh ones.

A famous poet did not teach his children Welsh and a leading playwright used the Welsh Not in his classes. It was time, too, when harsher methods were sincerely used and approved to mould children and discourage what were considered to be bad habits. Cruel techniques were used to 'correct' a child's left-handedness, for example. Pleased indeed must have been the teacher who, by well-meant ridicule and torture, rid pupils of Welshness and left-handedness.

In the 1880s, when Mrs Roberts was going to school, neither English language teaching nor the Welsh Not had reached her part of Lleyn. She left school at thirteen without a word of English and she said to me, 'As you can see, I have managed quite well without it for more than ninety years.' In those far-off days she lived a life in the traditional mould of rural Wales, fashioned by school, chapel, *eisteddfod* and the land. She took a piece of bread to school for lunch and asked farmers for butter-milk to go with it. On Sundays there was 'nothing done that was not ordained by the chapel . . . my mother would not permit any work on a Sunday in our house. How things have changed today.' Mrs Roberts worked as a housekeeper at a large farm, later married a farmer and had five children. Some of the Welsh monoglots like to imply that they know more English

than they can in fact speak: it is an echo of the days when
Welsh was being humbled and possession of English made you,
apparently, a citizen of the world. Mrs Roberts, however, has
never been troubled by her lack of *Saesneg*—English. When her
children learned it, it was simply a school subject which was
occasionally useful to her when English forms had to be filled
in. She has travelled no further than Bangor, about forty miles
away, and England is but a hazy image, based on what she has
been told, or has heard about through the Welsh language radio
and television.

She echoed the remark made by a monoglot Welsh girl
to the writer George Borrow in his journey through Wales
in 1854: 'English? What use do we have for English here?'
She found it quite remarkable that she was in a last-of-the-
Mohicans situation and that her only language had declined
so much in her own lifetime. 'Those young people campaigning for the language, making all that fuss, they are dead
right.'

The old language of Wales, what Professor Tolkien called
the senior language of British civilization, remains one of
the country's least understood, most sensitive and most
squabbled-over facets. From England it appears foreign and
unpronounceable, as tongue-tying and baffling in appearance as Polish. It is widely believed that it exists only in
trace form, a funny lingo spoken by mountain people and
bards.

The language is a delicate and spiky subject for, like love, it is
a deep matter of the mind or the soul and for many of those who
have it as their first language, it is not just a tool, but a part of
their being. It is bound up with emotion, contradiction, irony,
controversy and the conflict of identity. In a country where
argument is a folk tradition it is one of the endless debates. The
'language question' is everywhere, in all corners, all strata of
Welsh life. It is unavoidable.

In one sense Welsh is the mainspring, the most potent force
of Welsh life, the expression of the Welsh heart, yet three-
quarters of the people do not speak it. People observe with
despair and rage its decline—and when they take action
they are praised as heroes on one side, branded as fanatics on

the other. The language is declining and pessimism is to be found everywhere, yet it is clearly and vigorously alive. It is deeply loved, yet also loathed. It is useless, but also important and vital. It should be a great force for unity, but it frequently divides. Some Welsh-speakers care very little for the future of their language. Some English-speakers who cannot understand its words, but understand something of its mystery, champion its cause. It enjoys bad will and good will. But I suppose that a majority of the 2,700,000 people of Wales are indifferent to it.

Languages, Dr Johnson remarked, are the pedigrees of nations, and, to a considerable extent the history of Wales is the history of its language. Welsh has a distinguished pedigree which stretches back fifteen centuries.

Its immediate ancestor was the British language. During the fifth and sixth centuries British changed and the Welsh language developed. By the eighth century it was a written language and, in basics, not very different from Welsh today. For many centuries the language was spoken widely in what is now Shropshire, Herefordshire and Gloucestershire.

The language retreated very slowly as English influence grew, and the first important wound was inflicted by the centralizing policies of the Tudors. The Welshman Henry Tudor, Henry VII, gained the English throne and the Red Dragon flag flew in London. His exploits thrilled the Welsh people and gave the illusion that ancient prophecies had been fulfilled.

But the Wales that the Tudors took over was a complex legal mess, a spaghetti of small territories, each with its own way of running its courts and administration. Thomas Cromwell, Henry VIII's adviser, took eight years to reorganize the administration of England and then turned his attention to the offending jumble of Wales.

Under the Laws in Wales Act of 1536, usually known as the Act of Union, and a more detailed Act of 1542, Wales and England were firmly stitched together. As it turned out the new laws dealt the Welsh language a great blow, which is why the lips of some Welshmen tighten at the mention of the Act of Union, but some historians maintain that this was not the king's intention. He wanted to abolish feudalism and did so by breaking up the old system and dividing Wales into shires for administrative convenience.

The laws also gave Welshmen a king's gift: political equality with Englishmen. For the convenience of uniformity, Welsh law was replaced by English law. The preamble to the Act of 1536 said that the people of Wales 'do daily use a speche nothing like ne consonaunt to the naturall mother tonge used within this Realme'. And it also said that the government wanted 'utterly to extirpe alle and singulare the sinister usages and customes' which were different from those in England. This phrase, 'utterly to extirpe,' is quoted quite frequently in an effort to demonstrate that the Act set out with evil intent, to smash Welsh. But there is a strong argument, based on a close reading of the preamble, that this is a wrong conclusion to draw, that the 'extirping' referred to the 'laws and customes' of Wales. Clause 20 of the Act, however, laid it on the line in the interests of uniformity . . . 'all Justices shall proclayme and kepe all courtes in the Englisshe tonge and also from hensforth no personne or personnes that use the Welsshe speche or langage shall have or enjoy any maner office or fees within the Realme of Englonde Wales or other Kinges dominions onles he or they use and exercise the speche or langage of Englisshe.'

Thus, to make his way in the brave new English world, the Welshman of ambition and learning had to know English and had to go to London to make his career. The Act of Union's threat to the language and, therefore, to the national life could hardly have been perceived by the people.

There was no sudden exodus. There was a cultural osmosis. The educated people, the aristocrats, the gentry, the middle class, who naturally administered through the courts and the civil service, gradually seeped away to where the careers were or, if they stayed, abandoned the Welsh language, now stripped of legal status and validity. The king's new deal released them from the burden of having to patronize the native culture and having to be stout defenders of the Welsh tradition. They began to graze the greener English grass and in a hundred years or so the top level of Welsh society had drifted so that there was a great linguistic and instinctive gulf between them and the ordinary people, the *gwerin*.

The Act of Union started a damaging brain drain, but, within a generation the Welsh language was thrown a lifeline. An Act of Parliament decreed that the Bible should be translated into Welsh: the aim was to ensure that the Welsh-speakers had an official Protestant Bible which would help them keep to that particular faith. The Act also ordered that an English Bible should be placed in every parish church, so that 'such as do not understand the language may, by conferring both tongues together, the sooner attain to the knowledge of the English tongue'. But, naturally, the Welsh-speaker was attracted more to the book he could understand. And this book, published in 1588 and a great improvement on an earlier turgid translation, quickly won its way into Welsh hearts. Set in the poetic tradition, its dignity and warmth were an inspiration and, as the standard and official work, it had prestige; it saved Welsh and, as the keystone of religious, community and educational life, ensured the survival of the language through the social turmoil of the nineteenth and early twentieth centuries.

It has, however, been a rough journey and there have been countless knocks. One of these, the report of a commission of inquiry into education in Wales published in 1847, was a hammer blow. If the intention of the authorities was to persuade the Welsh people that the native language was a millstone around the national neck, and to sting them into learning English, the report was a considerable success. Using the technique of a meld of part-truth and emotive phrase, well-known to propagandists, the report, compiled by three young barristers, was a condemnation of the language and of the Welsh people. It drew, with painstaking and painful detail, a black picture of the state of education in Wales. The Welsh language was said to distort the truth, favour fraud and abet perjury . . . to be the language of slavery, to keep the people isolated and beneath the hatches; moreover, the people were said to be ignorant and immoral.

There was a roar of rage when the report, in three blue volumes, was published. It was nicknamed '*brad y llyfrau gleision*'—the treason of the blue books—and although its

Anglican bias was attacked and its distortions exposed by writers, a lot of the mud stuck.

The industrialization of South Wales is blamed for assisting the erosion of Welsh and, certainly, the great number of Englishmen, and others, who came to work in the mines and ironworks contributed to the dilution of Welshness. The community that grew up in South Wales after the coalfield was opened up was never a homogeneous one. But industrialization also had a strengthening effect on the language. In Ireland the Irish language suffered severely by the break-up of the rural community and emigration in the nineteenth century. Hard conditions forced many people to leave farms and cottages in the Welsh countryside and, although more than 100,000 people quit Wales in the nineteenth century, a substantial loss for a small country, many families found they did not have to go too far. While many were moving to England, America, Australia, others moved to the valleys of the south and took with them their way of life and their language. The population grew and, of course, the number of Welsh-speakers increased. In the busy and booming valleys the chapels filled and developed a strong economic base and were more able to spread the religious and cultural message.

Sixty years ago the Rhondda and other valleys were strongly Welsh and in the Vale of Glamorgan the language was as strong as it is in Cardiganshire today. Even in 1951 more than half of the people living in the coalfield were registered as Welsh-speakers. But while the number of Welsh-speakers increased from the beginning of industrialization until the First World War, the proportion of them decreased. In 1891 there were nearly 889,000 Welsh-speakers (54·4 per cent of the population); in 1911 the number of Welsh-speakers reached a peak—977,000 (43·5 per cent); in 1961 656,000 (26 per cent).

There were, and are, myriad and complex factors in this decline: desertion by the gentry, the outlawing of Welsh from administration and courts for four centuries, inward and outward migration, the education system, and the fact that Welsh people were encouraged to deny it and regard it as the talk of the scullery, the patois of the yokel. Trade unionism dealt another blow because English became the medium for the

E

iron-strong union movement in Wales; 'mixed' marriages have also undermined the language because Welsh nearly always loses out when a bilingual person marries an English-only person; the strong influences of radio, and, in the last twenty years, television, have also eaten away at the roots of Welsh.

Old attitudes linger on. The proprietress of a small hotel in Caernarvonshire told me that for a few weeks in the summer she employed two young Welsh people, a youth and a girl, to help out in the kitchen and the dining room. 'The boy's mother came to me when I took him on and said that if I caught him speaking Welsh with the girl in front of the guests I was to give him a clout.'

One evening I stopped at a restaurant in Aberystwyth and took a table next to three people. They were a trio of the kind you often see in Aber'—a father, mother and their son or daughter who is at the university college. The parents have journeyed through the hinterland to visit the family's bright hope and buy him or her a square meal. These particular parents had ventured from Surrey and, with the wild fastness of Plynlimon mountain conquered, were listening to their daughter's talk of college life.

'I'm sharing a place with some Welsh girls; they talk all the time in Welsh.'

The mother's eyebrows arched and her spoonful of melon stopped at the mouth's brink. 'They speak Welsh?'

'Oh, mummy, they speak English as well. They're bilingual, you see. . . .'

'Well, dear, you know best, I'm sure, but Welsh. . . .'

It was as if she had just been told that her daughter's flat-mates had only lately given up head hunting.

The magistrate in a London court who exclaimed recently 'Welsh! I have never heard such nonsense,' when a man wanted to give evidence in Welsh, and the visitor who grinned and said 'It sounds like indigestion to me' were merely echoing what has been said up and down the years about the language. Thus a sniggering pamphlet of 1682: 'Their native gibberish is usually prattled through the whole of Taphydom except in their market towns, whose inhabitants being a little raised do begin to despise it. 'Tis usually cashiered out of gentlemen's houses . . . there may be some glimmering hopes that the British language may be quite extinct and may be English'd out of Wales.' Another pamphlet said Welsh was 'inarticulate and guttural and sounds more like the gobbling of geese or turkeys than the speech of rational creatures'. To some the matter of the language is easily resolved. 'If everyone speaks English what's all the fuss about?' they ask, washing their hands of the matter and sidestepping the issue.

The writer Gwyn Thomas, in his book *A Welsh Eye*, had this to say about the agitation on behalf of the language: 'We were not, in terms of nationality, a homogeneous people. Into the valleys had poured as many Englishmen as indigenous Welsh. The only binding things were indignity and deprivation. The Welsh language stood in the way of our fuller union and we made ruthless haste to destroy it. We nearly did.

'The tide of our final Radical rapture has drained away. The revival of the Welsh language has witnessed the most drastic contraction of dreams in the history of weariness. Whereas we and our fathers stood squarely on the proposition that we should raise to full stature all the human refuse on this earth at whatever expense in hernias, the national brain now bulges with such projects as the need to deny Welsh rainwater to the Liverpool water-board, and a demand that the present limited education we now give to our children in English should be replaced by an even more limited education in Welsh.'

It is a fact that many Welshmen agree with Matthew Arnold who wrote in *The Times* in 1866 that Welsh was 'the curse of Wales'. They believe his attack is just as valid more than a century later.

How many Welshmen are looking forward to dancing on the language's grave? 'I am, for one,' a Welsh-speaking Cardiffian assured me. 'If it wasn't for the newspapers and all the publicity, Welsh would have died a natural death long ago. The language is a barrier in the education of our children and to our total unity with the rest of Britain and all the benefits that brings. It will be far better when Welsh is out of the way and we all accept a language which is used and understood the world over. Why fret about a minority language, a second language (because everyone knows English) when there is the economy and unemployment to get sorted out. Let's be honest; worrying about the language is pure sentimentality. When it goes over the hill, and it will, I'll say good riddance.'

In the newsletter brought out for the staff of BBC Wales, the language question is debated from time to time, and here is one view expressed in a letter: 'At last someone has said publicly what many Welshmen have been saying privately for years now. Wales is populated by a vast majority of non-Welsh-speaking Welshmen: people who are as patriotically Welsh as the next man but who not only cannot speak Welsh but are angered by the efforts of a five per cent minority who wish to force their language—with all its dual-tongued street and town names and all the costs involved—on to the ninety-five per cent majority. . . . The main gulf between the people of Wales is that of language. And as the poet Mr Dic Jones said on BBC Wales recently, if the language does not stand on its own without artificial props, then it deserves to die.'

At a time when the Welsh Language Society was in the large headlines, through its demonstrations, this view appeared in a letter to the *Western Mail*: 'Of course a vast majority of Welsh-men are monoglot English-speaking. And these are the Welshmen who keep the wheels turning in industry and normal Welsh life. The law-breaking youths who brashly profess such nationalist tendencies have yet to regularly work and strive for the benefit of Wales. Their time seems spent only in destroying the Wales that the English-speaking Welshmen have built.'

Others feel differently. They believe Welsh is one of the great possessions of the British Isles, a fundamental part of the concept of Wales as a nation, the unique badge of an independent people. They have a saying—*Cenedl heb iaith: cenedl heb galon*. A nation without language: a nation without heart. They believe that without the existence of the language Wales would be just a geographic term, an historic capsule with a beginning and an end.

Some who do not possess Welsh wish that they did and feel positively deprived, or, at least, interested enough to do something about it. In their thousands they go to evening classes, learn Welsh through radio and television courses and buy language records and teach-yourself books. 'My parents spoke

Welsh but they never wanted me to learn it,' a friend said. 'They thought it was a bit second-rate. But I am earning my living in Wales and moving a lot in circles where Welsh is widely used. It makes me wish I could speak it; I'm not much good at languages and I feel I'm missing something.'

A journalist with his mind full of newly-learned verbs and mutations said: 'I'm a Welshman and it just seemed so ridiculous that I could not speak my native language. It's been on my conscience for years now. I'm enjoying learning it and I feel I'm recovering some lost territory.'

An acquaintance said: 'I learned Welsh as an adult and it took me twenty years to get fluent. If you ask what the motive was I suppose that the truth is that I felt humiliated that I did not possess my native language.'

Dafydd Williams, who is the secretary of the Welsh Nationalist Party, spent five years learning Welsh. 'I went to grammar school in Cardiff where they gave us Welsh lessons, but without much enthusiasm. Welsh was pushed into the background and history was English history. Of course, some of the boys at school knew Welsh and, frankly, I envied them. I wanted to know about my own country and be involved in its culture. I learned Welsh as an adult, starting with a radio course, and now that I'm fluent I feel connected with nearly twenty centuries of Welsh history. This is spiritually satisfying in itself: when I had no Welsh I had a sense of deprivation. But to be able to use the language as a part of my everyday life is even more rewarding. I feel complete and I didn't before.'

Dr Bobi Jones, the poet and novelist who learned Welsh as a young man, said in a magazine article: 'Why I write in Welsh is partly why I write at all: there is no longer any question to answer. Writing in Welsh means now to be in the middle of the great human struggle—not to have pulled out, not to be superior or neutral or to have one's eyes on the ends of the world as if they were not here; it is to be sensitive to the tingling life of words, to the rhythmic muscles of sentences, to the quiveringness of images, to the possession of great themes. It is to turn the soil in this part of the earth as it should really be turned.'

A sensitive analysis of attitudes to the Welsh language was

57

made by Professor T. J. Morgan, Professor of Welsh at the University of Wales College, Swansea, in a commentary on the Gittins Report on Primary Education in Wales. Welsh in schools, he wrote, was now highly charged with touchiness.

'Some of us, when the subject is mentioned, jump up to the position of alert, ready to defend, like a lioness protecting her cubs; and others get impatient and hostile and suspicious and are nasty about the words "Welsh essential". I am putting it in that way to bring out the squabbliness of the subject and its emotionalism and touchiness in order to emphasize that it is not a simple educational matter. If anything, it is a more highly charged subject than . . . the teaching of religion in school. Certain parts of the school curriculum are liable to generate feeling and controversy and odium and bitterness, and, we might as well admit it, Welsh has become that; proposals which imply a stepping-up in the teaching of Welsh in the schools are not going to be received and considered rationally but, rather, irrationally. The response to the proposals will be determined by prejudice, and not by reason; and quite often, even when rational or comprehensible arguments are used to oppose or resist the proposals, such as cost or usefulness, these are overt arguments to provide an intellectual justification for an attitude or behaviour which is in fact deep-seated and irrational or psychological.

'Those of us who are in favour of thorough-going and seriously-meant bilingualism are in favour not because we have been converted to this way of thinking. We start off with this belief and to us the desirability and reasonableness of this policy are self-evident. In our inquiry into motives we must realize that there are others among us who are incapable of thinking as we do, and to whom the desirability of this policy is not self-evident; and they have this attitude (most of them) as naturally and innocently as we have ours. How can we, who are conditioned in favour of a bilingual policy, win over the passive and innocently unconvinced? . . . each one of us would find it extremely hard to provide a rational argument why he or she should continue to exist; the urge to survive does not depend upon arguments and evidence for its own justification; the desire is its own justification. This concept of survival can be applied to the language, for in the make-up of many of us the language is an extension of ourselves.

'The educational system of the second half of the nineteenth century has been regarded as the main cause of the decline of Welsh in the modern period. I am not going to defend it, but I am not convinced that it is the main cause. . . . I find it difficult to attribute the decline to external factors and come back all the time to the admission I have to make, that the majority of the Welsh-speaking population have been Welsh-speaking and have transmitted Welsh to their children not for reasons of conviction but because it was innocently natural for them to do so; and because they lacked conscious conviction, they have been the innocent victims of the processes of erosion. Cultural awareness is a quality found only in a fraction of the population, and it is only in this fraction that one should reasonably expect a sense of concern for the fate of the language and its culture and to find strong convictions and an inner compulsion to defend the language. It is a mistake to attribute to the Welsh-speaking population *en masse* the convictions and motives possessed only by the element among them which has a cultural awareness and therefore a sense of urgency. But it is this bulk, which is innocently free from motives and convictions and a sense of urgency and emergency, that needs to be cajoled or roused and won over, for it will never do to follow a policy of cutting one's losses and relying for the survival of the language upon the limited class of the culturally aware.'

In spite of the cultural teredo worms and the psychological warfare, the Welsh language today enjoys a vigorous life and, certainly, a more varied one than it ever has. It is by no means 'English'd out of Wales' and, if it is dying, economic forces and electronics notwithstanding, it is going to be a very long death-bed scene indeed. For many thousands it is the first language, the one in which they weave their thoughts, the language of home, school, courtship, social contact, cultural expression and commerce.

Many jobs in Wales require Welsh as a qualification, a fact that leads to growls of 'apartheid' and complaints that Welsh-speakers are trying to perpetuate a clique. But many of those who make this complaint are also in the ranks of those who say

Welsh is useless and should be allowed to die because it has no economic value. The ability to speak Welsh is obviously an advantage in certain jobs, particularly in those areas where the people are using Welsh as their first language. Most policemen in North Wales, for example, are Welsh-speakers and the language is regarded as a desirable qualification for new entrants, although those without it are not barred. Government departments, post offices and banks tend to reflect the extent of the Welsh-speaking in the area they serve because the staff live locally. About 15,000 of the 21,000 teachers working in Wales can speak Welsh and it has been estimated that about 8000 of them are in posts where the language is essential. About a quarter of the BBC's staff of 830 in Wales have to know Welsh and about fifteen per cent of Harlech Television's staff of 300 have to know it.

Because of the pressure applied, both noisily and quietly, Welshmen have regained the right, after 400 years, to use Welsh in the courts. The language has equal validity with English under the provisions of the Welsh Language Act and about 400 official forms are available either in Welsh or in Welsh and English. The Welsh-speaking community has access to a considerable storehouse of literature, a steady output of new books from a small and dedicated publishing industry, seven newspapers, a variety of magazines and about twenty-five hours a week of radio and television broadcasts.

How long can the vigour of the language last? It is recognized that education must play the major part if Welsh is to have a future life of any relevance. Education is a delicate matter anywhere and natural concern leads some parents to become education experts the moment their child enters school. In Wales, where education has traditionally been more highly regarded than in many parts of England, and where the Welsh language has to be considered, prejudices lie a little more thickly on the ground.

Englishmen may wonder, from afar, why Welsh language teaching is such a sensitive business. But it is not just another subject. It lies in a web of emotional and political feelings and is inevitably something of a battleground where bigotry sometimes intrudes.

'It's these nationalists,' a father of two primary school children fumed. 'They make me sick with their demands for more Welsh. Why do my kids have to sit through Welsh lessons just because these fanatics hold the reins?'

The *South Wales Echo* reported in the summer of 1971 that some parents at the Glamorgan village of Sully were protesting about a bilingual education project that had been introduced in the village school. This subsequent letter from a reader is typical of the way that some people in Wales feel about Welsh in the schools:

'What a brave stand of the Sully parents opposed to the bilingual education project. They are to be admired for their fight against the insidious extension of compulsory teaching of the Welsh language.

'I am pleased to see that some are prepared to fight against this encroachment upon the previously soundly based education of the children of English-speaking Welshmen. This unfair bias in favour of Welsh-speaking minorities is so strong in education. Unfortunately it is even stronger in broadcasting.

'Certain Welsh-speaking fanatics wield disproportionate power in high places.

'Unless the general public in Wales is quickly alerted to this danger then the freedom of the large majority of Welshmen will be quickly eroded.'

Certainly there are a few parents who shrink from Welsh in education as if it were a kind of cultural leprosy. 'I just couldn't believe it,' a father confided with a shake of his head. 'I went to pick her up from school and she was talking to her little pal half in Welsh and half in English.' It is fair to say that while prejudice exists at both extremes of the issue of Welsh in education, there is, in the reasonable and middle ground, a large body of parents who have only good will for Welsh and want their children to learn it, although they do not have the language themselves.

The bilingual education project, which started in 1968, and has recently been extended because of its success, is showing how the Welsh language can be re-seeded even in those very large corners of Wales which once looked as if they would be for ever English. The project started in twenty-five carefully

61

selected primary schools throughout anglicized Wales and at first involved children aged from five to seven. They lived half their school day through English and the remaining half through Welsh. Young children, of course, learn languages very easily. Those in the bilingual experiment absorb Welsh unconsciously, as they absorb English, through their activities of painting, modelling, playlets, games and songs. Education psychologists and language teachers recognize that about the age of seven or eight a child becomes aware of language, of grammar, of the need to translate.

'Catching the children young, well before they reach the language barrier, has been the secret of the bilingual project's success,' Mr Elwyn Richards, the project director, told me. 'The children become natural and instant translators and build up a large vocabulary. It is painless language teaching and there is nothing formal about it at all.'

The significant point is that the children who so rapidly become bilingual are from English-speaking homes and that Welsh is not just another school subject but a teaching medium. Many children in Wales get compulsory Welsh lessons at school but, as with all languages, only those with flair have any chance of becoming bilingual as a result of this traditional method. Most children forget it when they leave school and retain a few phrases, in the same way that people in England store some unused and rusting French and German.

The bilingual project draws on the experience gained in the past decade in the bilingual schools, known as Welsh schools, which have shown that children from English-speaking homes can derive a rich educational experience from learning through Welsh. Indeed, many children have gone on to do much of their learning through their second tongue. They study the sciences through English, but are taught languages like French and German through the medium of Welsh, and take their GCE examinations in these subjects through Welsh.

In the autumn of 1971 the bilingual experiment, which is costing £100,000, was widened considerably to take in more infants' schools and to include children aged seven to eleven in some primary schools. It was given four more years to run and should it achieve with older children what it has achieved with

62

the very young, the system could be adopted very widely in Wales.

Mr Richards said: 'All Welshmen have to make up their minds about the language. They can decide to oppose it, to tolerate it, or to support it. It is reassuring to find so many parents behind us. Our job is not to save the Welsh language whatever the cost, but we believe we have an attractive method for achieving bilingualism—and that opens the door for all children in Wales to another culture, a heritage and richer life.

'Welsh, in my view, cannot be kept alive by retreating to the mountains or by existing in communes. It must live a vigorous and valid life alongside English. The battle for it will therefore be won in the strongly anglicized areas, like Glamorgan. I would say that this project is our last chance to achieve a genuine bilingualism in Wales. Twenty years from now it would be too late. That shows how critical the situation is.'

Suspicious parents worry that this kind of Welsh teaching may in some way damage their children's education prospects. 'But no education authority or teacher would stand for that,' Mr Richards said, 'particularly in Wales where we have a reputation for good education. Whatever the language they are hearing the children are always making progress. There are certain bonuses, too. Teachers find they can explain certain concepts more effectively in Welsh, children learn to read it more quickly because it is phonetic and easier than English, and children of a lower IQ who would not normally get even the chance of learning a second language have no trouble in learning Welsh this natural way. Moreover, it has been noticed that there has been an improvement in the standard of English because children develop a greater feel for language, for the raw material of words. Concern nearly always evaporates when the parents see how Welsh is taught. A report to the Schools Council on the attitudes of parents whose children were involved in the bilingual project, said: "Although there was some opposition in some areas at the start this has now disappeared and we have many reports of enthusiastic support from those who once opposed the project." Dialogue, of course, is the best weapon when you encounter prejudice.'

The Secretary of State for Wales made an important speech

to the Welsh Joint Education Committee in July of 1971 when he stressed that compulsory teaching of Welsh in the secondary schools could create hostility towards the language. 'We cannot in a democratic society compel anyone to learn anything. For some parents Welsh is a burning issue and as the home has the most significant effect on a child's learning at school, Welsh cannot be effectively taught when the home is hostile to it. It would be better to teach Welsh effectively in a smaller number of schools with adequate resources and full parental backing, rather than teach it ineffectively in a larger number of schools where teachers and parents may be indifferent and hostile. The teaching of Welsh should be strongly supported where it is still a vital cultural element.'

Well, there is certainly hostility in some homes, and indifference in many more. Some cynics say that for English-speaking parents to have a Welsh-speaking child is something of a *cachet* in smart middle-class neighbourhoods and, indeed, Welsh is achieving a certain trendiness in some small English circles. All the same, most teachers believe that the majority of parents send their children to the Welsh language schools from sincere motives.

There has even been a small Welsh revival in education in Monmouthshire, once a tennis-ball county between England and Wales, but now officially a Welsh one. The county gave in to apathy and stopped teaching Welsh more than forty years ago, but now there are two flourishing Welsh language primary schools and a number of Welsh play groups. The demand for this facility came from parents who moved from Welsh-speaking districts to find work at the steelworks near Newport and from English-speakers who wanted their children to have access to a rich culture.

The pattern of Welsh language teaching varies considerably throughout Wales. Accurate information about the situation is difficult to collect because no central authority collates it, which is rather surprising in view of the public interest in the subject. What does emerge from an examination of the scene is that in many areas Welsh is an obligatory subject but in others Welsh instruction is difficult to obtain.

Of the 483,000 children in the maintained schools of Wales,

about 8000, less than two per cent, are in the forty-seven bilingual schools and departments and are being taught mainly in Welsh. But several thousands more are being educated in Welsh to a large degree in the strongly Welsh areas.

Glamorgan, although thoroughly anglicized has more Welsh-speakers than any other county. It has a policy aimed at making the county bilingual by the end of the century. And most of those concerned for Welsh would be happy if all the education authorities of Wales had Glamorgan's policy. Glamorgan children have to learn Welsh until they are eleven, and afterwards, depending on their school, it is compulsory until they are twelve, thirteen or fourteen. In Cardiff and Swansea the language is an essential part of the curriculum until the age of thirteen. In Merioneth, Cardiganshire and Carmarthenshire, Welsh is compulsory from infant school to the age of fifteen or up to GCE Ordinary level. It is compulsory from the age of five, or seven, depending on the district, up to thirteen, in Anglesey, Caernarvonshire, Montgomeryshire, Denbighshire and Flintshire. Pembrokeshire has worked out a compromise: the northern part of the county is Welsh-speaking and the education policy is that Welsh is compulsory from the time a child starts school until he has completed two years at secondary school. In south Pembrokeshire, 'England beyond Wales', where little Welsh is spoken, the language is not compulsory but some classes are provided at the request of parents. In Radnorshire there is no Welsh taught in the primary schools and it is a subject at only one of the five secondary schools.

The 1967 Gittins Report on Primary Education in Wales maintained that the only way to keep Welsh alive was to organize a bilingual educational system, but added that it should not be compulsory. The Schools Council is acting on some of the other recommendations of the report, spending a quarter of a million pounds on the development of bilingual education in anglicized areas and a study of the attitudes of children, parents and teachers to the learning of Welsh, which should be very revealing.

The people at the receiving end of the educational activity have not so far provided the kind of figures that those who look to education for encouragement would like to see. In 1970, of all the GCE ordinary level candidates only one person in seven took Welsh and only one in sixteen took it at advanced level. More school children take French in GCE than take Welsh.

Nevertheless there are hopeful signs elsewhere, particularly in the success of the bilingual project. Compared with the situation a few years ago, more Welsh children today are able to get an insight into their heritage and culture through the language.

In more than 700 schools of Wales are branches of the re- markable patriotic youth movement called *Urdd Gobaith Cymru*. Its magazines, graded for natural Welsh-speakers and for learners, are distributed through the schools because they are regarded as important teaching aids and the movement receives £20,000 a year in grants from local authorities.

The *Urdd*—its name is translated as the Welsh League of Youth—is a vital carapace for Welsh values. In its fifty years of life it has been such an important influence that, without its existence, the language and culture would now be in a much weaker condition. The movement puts Wales first: its members are pledged to serve Wales, their fellow men and Christ. Being unashamedly patriot-nationalist, it has often had to walk a tightrope between patriotism and pure politics. Cynics growl that it is a training organization for nationalists, but the long- standing respectability and good intentions of the *Urdd* enable it to work closely with the education authorities.

In 1969, the *Urdd* was faced with the most worrying dilemma of its history. It was invited to be represented at the investiture of Prince Charles at Caernarvon. This event was regarded by a section of the Welsh public as an extravagant and embarrassing political stunt and acceptance of the invitation would have caused a very damaging split in the movement. Refusal would have made the movement look churlish and narrow-minded in the eyes of other Welsh people. In the end the *Urdd* compro- mised, refusing to be associated with the carnival and cere- monial at Caernarvon, but welcomed the prince to its training centre the day after the investiture.

The *Urdd* has more than 45,000 members aged between eight and twenty-five and more than 1000 branches. Its seven maga- zines have an annual circulation of more than half a million.

The movement works to encourage an awareness of the heritage of Wales among young people and to reveal to those who do not speak the Welsh language some of the richness of the culture. It therefore ignites and keeps alive the sense of national identity in many young people and forms a link between North and South, and English and Welsh Wales. The movement reflects the language pattern and many thousands of its members are those who have English as their mother-tongue. Summer camps and training courses with a strong 'outward bound' flavour are a large feature of the *Urdd* activities. Everything—sailing, canoeing, climbing, rambling, camp-fire talk, meals—has a Welsh language emphasis. Many young people have their first contact with Welsh musical and literary expression in the movement's clubs and concerts and at the rehearsals for the *Urdd eisteddfod*, one of the important events of the Welsh cultural year. Like most youth movements the *Urdd* sets great store by social work and its members help and entertain the elderly, sick and handicapped.

The movement has its spiritual root in those Welsh school-rooms of the nineteenth century where the Welsh Not was used. Owen Edwards, who became a chief inspector of education for Wales, was one of the children who wore the Welsh Not and the experience was branded in his mind. He later became convinced that Welsh children should know more of Wales and its heritage and started a magazine for them. He wrote and published it for thirty years and the writing was done in an informal style of Welsh that children readily appreciated, and the style itself was pioneering in that it broke away from the rather stiff chapel-Welsh and demonstrated that the language could have a brighter life in print. Edwards's son, Sir Ifan ab Owen Edwards, carried on the magazine and, through it, founded *Urdd Gobaith Cymru*.

One of the facets of the Welsh language world which shines most brightly within the *Urdd* is pop music. It is barely known in England and, indeed, in some parts of Wales, that the young people of Wales are sustaining a thriving Welsh language folk and pop music business. A few years ago the very idea would have been laughed at, but today there is a strong following supporting five record companies, a weekly radio show and

67

television show, crowded concerts, even fan clubs and a 'Top Ten' column in *Y Cymro*, the leading Welsh language newspaper. Most groups and singers are amateurs, but a few are professionals.

In essence, Welsh pop is not an imitation of the kind of Anglo-American pop that is associated in the minds of old people over the age of twenty-five with shuddering beats, great noise, screaming singers and a baffling weirdness. It is true that some Welsh pop groups merely copy American pop and put in a Welsh translation or substitution for the original words. At best this sounds passingly piquant. But if translation of the imported fodder was all that Welsh pop was about, it could never have got off the ground.

It is still young and a fair proportion of it is bland and frankly church-hall and talent-content. A little of it is junk. But the best Welsh pop is important because it is interesting and tuneful and says a good deal about the way that young people in Wales feel about life, events and the condition of their country. It is, essentially, homegrown. Increasingly, the writers of the best songs are drawing on the tradition of poetry and find inspiration in the works of famous bards and in the *Mabinogion*, the collection of Arthurian legends, which is one of the treasures of Welsh literature. Some of the lyrics are spiky and ironic and many, making a direct appeal to the Welsh soul, tend to be romantic, nostalgic or sad and are about love and Wales. Whereas Anglo-American pop is regarded by many young people as their special property, is fenced off with jargon and attitudes, and is viewed by older people with pain or incomprehension, Welsh pop is usually acceptable to the younger generation's parents.

In a country where the political antennae are sensitively tuned, producers of Welsh pop shows have to listen carefully to the lyrics of the songs, and sometimes a verse or two is deleted. Producers and performers recognize that there is a tightrope to be walked. A BBC television producer said: 'The songs that are the targets for criticism are not political in the normal sense. They are patriotic—and there is a distinction. It is natural for Welsh people to sing about their country and their love for it. It is a pity that some people are upset by this.'

Political antennae are particularly sensitive when Dafydd

Iwan appears on television. He is one of the most popular of the Welsh language singers and it is natural that he should appear regularly. At the same time he is a leading member of the Welsh Language Society and is, to say the least, a controversial man. People who see him on the screen sometimes reflect that members of the society have occupied broadcasting buildings in demonstrations on behalf of the campaign for a Welsh television channel, and that Dafydd Iwan himself has been in the news frequently as a result of language campaigns and has been fined and imprisoned for his language activities.

The standard of records produced in Wales has steadily improved. Cambrian Recordings, the largest of the Welsh record companies, is making more than 200,000 discs a year, of which about 135,000 are Welsh pop. The remainder are of traditional Welsh choirs and tenors, for which there is a steady demand. In those areas where the language is strong about a third of the total sales in some record shops is of Welsh records and, when a particularly popular Welsh record comes out, the sales temporarily outstrip the sales of English discs.

The growth of Welsh pop music is a part of the changing attitude of a section of Welsh youth and of the increasing awareness of the language issue. The golden age of the Welsh choirs whose voices thundered from Cardiff to Caernarvon, enough to rattle the bones of St David himself, may have faded, but the songs are still there. It is simply that the melody and the rhythm and the motivation have changed.

Although the Welsh pop shows on television have their small circle of English-speaking admirers, the usual reaction to them in most English-speaking homes in Wales is to take the action always employed when a Welsh programme comes on: switch off or switch over. The BBC in Wales and HTV, the independent television company, have to provide services in both languages but many English-speakers become annoyed when confronted by a Welsh programme and many Welsh-speakers regard the number of hours of Welsh language broadcasting as derisory. Broadcasting, in fact, has become one of the major cockpits of the Welsh language campaign.

The BBC motto says that nation shall speak peace unto nation, but when the speech is Welsh the television lamps start going out all over Wales in the homes where it is not understood.

When the speech is English and the quality of the programme is mediocre, the cultural teeth start to grind. The BBC, which is a prime target, is regarded by one side as a nationalist-oriented organization, biased towards the Welsh language, which insists on broadcasting, at peak times, programmes that only the Welsh-speaking minority can understand. It is regarded by the other side as part of the 'cultural imperialist set-up' eroding the Welsh language; it is the 'British Brainwashing Corporation' of slogan and demo fame.

The BBC and HTV are in the unenviable position of having to attempt to please everyone in what is often an emotional situation. Bearing in mind the complexities and technical limitations, they do an excellent job. They have an obligation to ensure that Welsh-speakers can see good programmes at peak times. In the old days, when Welsh was pushed to the very end of the evening, people used to telephone the BBC and demand, with some justice:

'What the hell do you think we are—bloody owls?'

On the other hand, when BBC Wales opts out of the network to show a Welsh programme, English-speakers, particularly newcomers to Wales like the growing number of retired people, are pained to discover that they cannot see, say, *The Andy Williams Show*. Still, television has helped to bring home the fact that Wales is a country of two languages and perhaps that is not such a bad thing.

BBC Wales produces about seven hours of Welsh language television programmes every week and Harlech Television (HTV) about six hours. They have an arrangement under which they do not transmit their Welsh programmes simultaneously. But even so there are many Welsh-speakers who feel there is just not enough Welsh on the screens and are campaigning for a separate Welsh channel. BBC Wales head of programmes, Mr Owen Edwards, cares deeply for Welsh—his father was Sir Ifan ab Owen Edwards, founder of the *Urdd*—but he does not believe that the BBC's function is to be a preserving jar for the language.

'We have to serve all of Wales,' he said, 'and Wales is not

70

650,000 Welsh-speakers, nor the English-speakers who make up three-quarters of our population. It is everybody. We have to provide programmes in Welsh and in English because we are a bilingual network. We are not missionaries for the Welsh language. We could increase the number of Welsh language programmes, but we are concerned about the overall quality of the service. Welsh-speakers will certainly not watch programmes just because they are in Welsh. The thing that counts is quality and Welsh programmes have to be at least as good as English ones. They have to compete. And they must not be introverted. It is no good if they look just at Wales. They have to be outgoing, looking at the world, in an interesting fashion.'

Today, Welsh-speakers get radio and television programmes of good quality—the quantity is an altogether different matter. And they are getting books of a higher standard, both in terms of writing and of production, than they had only a few years ago.

Welsh language literature is supported by more than £80,000 a year of public money and the number of books published in Welsh is increasing. It now runs to about 130 titles a year. Books of poetry generally do better than novels: a popular novel might sell up to 1000 copies in its first year, while a book of poetry might sell 1500. The figures are small and they give an idea of the problem and the odds. Most Welsh-speakers get their Welsh books through libraries and it is reckoned that only 10,000 of the Welsh-speaking population of 650,000 buy a Welsh book occasionally—and only 2000 buy one as often as once a month.

This helps to explain why there is such reliance on public subsidy. The publishers are producing very small numbers of books and the relative cost of producing each volume is high. Because the market is so small it has not, until quite recently, been thought worthwhile to produce Welsh paperbacks. But in 1971 the firm of Gwasg Gomer published three, and there are hopes that more will be appearing in bookshops in the future.

There are about a dozen firms publishing Welsh books. But not for the profits. They rely on other printing work for their main income and produce Welsh books, with the aid of a subsidy, out of a love for, and a sense of duty towards, the Welsh language. And for a certain prestige.

Welsh newspapers share with the publishing trade the problems of a small market and high costs. But they, of course, get no public money.

The circulation of all the newspapers is probably less than 40,000. There is no Welsh language daily and the half-dozen weekly newspapers survive, in the main, because they are part of a group, like *Y Cymro*, the leading paper, and *Yr Herald Cymraeg* and *Herald Mon*, or are subsidized by the printing work done by their proprietors. These are not easy times for the Welsh papers. They could do with a lot more advertising. One of the most famous, *Baner ac Amserau Cymru*, has had to appeal for donations to keep going.

# 5 The last battle

On the evening of 13 February 1962 a lecture was broadcast in the BBC Welsh Home Service. It was in Welsh and it was called *Tynged yr Iaith*—The Fate of the Language—and was heard by several thousand people. Today we can see that that broadcast was a landmark in the modern history of Wales and the key to much of what is happening now. It came to be regarded by one section of the people as a courageous call to action and, by others, as a shrewd and mischievous incitement. From that forty-five minute broadcast sprang the movement which is fighting the last battle for the Welsh language. Behind the microphone, speaking in an incisive and scholarly voice was a small man of sixty-nine called Mr Saunders Lewis.

Because of the mood of the time, the increasing awareness of Welsh values among younger people and a gradually mounting, but rather vague, concern at what was happening to the Welsh language, some of the people of Welsh Wales were ready for action. The concern, however, was largely latent. The fuel was ready in the fireplace: all it needed was a spark and a draught. With his broadcast Saunders Lewis provided them.

Those who did not hear the lecture were soon told about it. Within a few months a group of students formed *Cymdeithas yr Iaith Gymraeg*—the Welsh Language Society. Within a few years, largely because activists polarized views, stirred consciences on one side and inflamed tempers on the other, the Welsh language had become one of the major social and political issues in Welsh life.

Clearly, *Tynged yr Iaith* was no ordinary radio lecture. Why did it have such great reverberations? The short answer is that Saunders Lewis, a man of great influence, touched the souls of some of the people of Wales, particularly the young. For he is not merely a remarkable writer. He is one of the great men of Welsh history and there is a section of Welsh youth which venerates him as a prophet. Some say he is the most eminent of patriotic Welshmen since the fifteenth century warrior prince

Owain Glyndwr. For half a century his voice has spoken for a Welsh dream. His has been one of the powerful voices of Welsh consciousness and a major influence in the cultural, literary and nationalist-political life of Wales. In 1925 Saunders Lewis and others formed *Plaid Cymru*, the Welsh Nationalist Party; he became its first president and, with a lecture at Machynlleth, which was published as the party's first pamphlet, he set out *Plaid Cymru*'s political philosophy. In it he said: 'Extremism is a ready danger to every moment . . . there are great dangers in hotheaded and unlimited nationalism. Fight for the essentials and do not go to extremes.' As the architect of modern Welsh nationalism he translated the then loose patriotic feelings of Wales into words and action and organization. Like Owain Glyndwr he breathed life into the dimming embers of Welsh national pride.

In the academic field he is rated the best Welsh dramatist, scholar and poet, an outstanding critic and, in his time, a remarkable teacher. He is regarded as a major European writer: his outlook is European and he has always presented Wales and its culture in a European, rather than a British, context. His plays usually have historical or Biblical themes and explore moral dilemmas. His work is translated into several languages and is well known in Italy, France and Spain. On St David's Day 1971, the *Academi Gymreig*, the society of Welsh writers, recommended him for a Nobel Prize in literature. He resists English—'English invades the whole of Welsh life'—reads it very little and writes in it hardly at all. Thus it is hardly surprising that one of the great writers of Wales is barely known in England.

Saunders Lewis does not have the kind of traditional Welsh background one might expect. He is not out of the mould of valley community, chapel, *eisteddfod* and the rest. The son of a minister, he was born in Wallasey in 1893, into a Welsh-speaking home, and went to Liverpool University. He volunteered for war service in 1914, was commissioned in the South Wales Borderers and was wounded. After the war he studied for his M.A., became a librarian in Glamorgan and wrote his first play. In 1923 he went to University College, Swansea, as a lecturer in Welsh, and became converted to Roman Catholicism, his wife's faith. It was no small achievement for a wartime army officer, a connoisseur of wine and a Roman Catholic to succeed in leading and dominating, from 1926 to 1939, a nationalist party which largely reflected nonconformist attitudes to Catholicism and temperance.

In Wales Saunders Lewis is not known only for his literary achievements and his political work. He is remembered, too, for one dramatic blow he struck for Wales, the impact of which has rung steadily down the years.

In 1936 the government agreed to build a bombing school for the Royal Air Force. The first site chosen, at Abbotsbury in Dorset, was spared after protests about the effect on the bird life. The second choice, land on the coast of Northumberland, was also spared after protests on conservation grounds. The third choice was Penyberth, in the Lleyn peninsula of Caernarvonshire, a Welsh-speaking district strong in the Welsh tradition.

A great protest movement got under way. Not a unanimous one because local people saw the chance of jobs at the bombing school. But, on cultural, nationalist and pacifist grounds, people throughout Wales joined the protest. It failed. Baldwin, the Prime Minister, said he did not see the point of receiving a deputation. In the interest of the defence of the realm, work on the bombing school went ahead. The people anxious for employment approved. The protesters smarted.

From Wales the London government appeared as the bloody-minded English, arrogant, narrow and indifferent to Welsh values and the character of the rural community. Among a few the feeling hardened that this was no time for impotent raging and gloomy poems.

On the night of 7 September 1936, Saunders Lewis, with D. J. Williams, a Fishguard schoolmaster and short story writer, and the Rev. Lewis Valentine, a Baptist Minister from North Wales, crept into the bombing school and set fire to some wooden buildings. They walked away from the blaze, which caused about £3000 worth of damage and, in the small hours, with the smell of smoke on their clothing, gave themselves up at Pwllheli police station.

Saunders Lewis handed over a letter in which the three

acknowledged responsibility: '. . . we have taken the only way left to us by a government contemptuous of the nation of Wales. . . .'

The burning of the bombing school made a deep impression on young nationalists and remains a symbolic and thrilling episode for many young people in Wales. The establishment and the older people were appalled, and some complained bitterly about the effect of the 'sabotage' on employment prospects (although in the end the fact that the area was prone to sea-fog made it unsuitable for a bombing school).

What made many people ponder was that here was a group of men, mature men (Lewis and Valentine were forty-two and Williams fifty-one), who had not conformed to the fashionable mass and materialist thinking. They had been willing to make a sacrifice, to strike a blow for Wales, for their ideals, for the then rather curious notion of Welsh self-respect. A small part of Wales had punched back.

At Caernarvonshire Assizes, where the three stood trial, Saunders Lewis referred to the authorities' demolition of Penyberth farmhouse which had had associations with pilgrims, poetry and Owain Glyndwr: 'The preservation of the harmonious continuity of the Welsh rural tradition of Lleyn, unbroken for fourteen hundred years, is for us a matter of life and death. . . . [The farmhouse] was a thing of hallowed and secular majesty. It was taken down and utterly destroyed a week before we burnt on its fields the timbers of the vandals who destroyed it and I claim that the people who ought to be in this dock are the people responsible for the destruction of Penyberth farmhouse. [Its] destruction . . . is typical and symbolic. The development of the bombing range at Lleyn into the inevitable arsenal it will become will destroy this essential home of Welsh culture, idiom and literature. It will shatter the spiritual basis of the Welsh nation.'

The theme of this speech was to be echoed again and again in Wales during the sixties and seventies.

Before the jury retired to decide, Saunders Lewis said to them: 'If you find us not guilty you declare your conviction as judges in this matter that the moral law is supreme; you declare that the moral law is binding on governments just as it is on private citizens. You declare that necessity of state gives no right to set morality aside, and you declare that justice, not material force, must rule in the affairs of nations.'

The jury failed to agree. The authorities, of course, wanted the matter decided on the facts, not motives: the case was sent for retrial at the Old Bailey where a jury of Londoners, with no emotional commitment, would bring a guilty verdict. The three men spoke in Welsh and Saunders Lewis made his attitude clear at once. 'I do not intend to defend myself in this court, the authority of which I cannot recognize in the trial of this cause because it has been transferred from my own country.' The three men were sentenced to nine months' imprisonment. In the four months between the two trials Saunders Lewis had written for the BBC one of his most famous plays, *Buchedd Garmon*, which contained an allegorical passage about a vineyard and the invasion of it by swine.

My country of Wales is a vineyard, given into my keeping,
To be handed down to my children and my children's
children
As an inheritance for all time.
And look, the pigs are rushing in to despoil it.

After their sentences, Williams returned to his school and Valentine to his religious work. But Saunders Lewis, in a shabby episode, was dismissed from his lecturing post by the University of Wales.

For fourteen years the gifted teacher could not get a worthwhile teaching post in his own country. For a time he taught in a Roman Catholic seminary, continued his literary work and supported his family by writing. He would not write in English; had he done so he might have had a more comfortable time. But he existed on the small fees paid by Welsh publications and knew hardship that sometimes amounted to poverty. He resigned the presidency of the nationalist party in 1939, saying he believed the fact that he was a Roman Catholic might damage the party. He quit active politics during the war, withdrawing to concentrate on his creative work, scholarship and criticism. Today he is a remote figure, seeing few visitors, but his influence remains immense and his articles and commentaries on the Welsh scene are eagerly read.

Such a man could hardly be universally loved in Wales. More than one father has told his son: 'Don't mention that man's name in this house.' Many Welshmen have treated him coldly; he has endured social and academic ostracism. He is a controversial and sometimes spiky man of steely intellect and even his friends and admirers have found his burning idealism and unbending honesty irritating on occasions.

I went to see him at his home in Penarth, a seaside town near Cardiff. Although he was then nearly seventy-eight, this diminutive man with a sharp-featured face and bright, penetrating eyes, was mowing his front lawn with a furious energy. He was in old pinstriped trousers, black jacket and white openneck shirt. I had been told to prepare myself for an encounter with a prickly character, but he was courtesy personified. In his study he poured sherry. It was not the normal question-and-answer interview. I asked him one general question about the condition of Wales and he talked at length, with great precision and without pause.

About the language question, he said: 'No nation ever understood another nation. It is impossible for Englishmen to feel for Welsh tradition, civilization and unity. That is merely human.

'Now I have a tremendous admiration for the men and women of the Welsh Language Society. They are fighting for what is the essence of Welsh nationalism and they are not fighting against England and the English, they are fighting the most unpopular battle of all: against their own people. They are fighting for what is the very lifeblood of Wales and the sadness is that their persecutors are the Welsh people on the councils and the magistrates' benches. Wales is a nation in subjection and unfortunately happy in its subjection. I would emphasize very much that the great opposition to Welsh nationalism does not come from England: the opposition is Wales and that is the tragedy of Wales after 400 years of subjection.

'The only real reason for nationalism, it seems to me, is the preservation of our civilization and values. The loss of the

78

language is the loss of an identity; it is the loss of a complete history and culture to the person concerned. Now it is very difficult to say all this to the proletariat in Wales because all education now, as well as the development of industry, ignores that side of life. We have a technological civilization and the importance of personality and cultural history is minimal.

'It is against this background that the Welsh language supporters are waging their campaign. It is a difficult situation. Once people have lost the language they object to anyone else having it. To make what they have lost important, to give it status, is therefore like a slap in the face. There is among the people of South Wales, in particular, an immense consciousness of not being English and, at the same time, of having thrown away the badge of their Welshness, their language. And inevitably they are driven to be more at one with the people of England. That is the only defence they have left.'

In his famous broadcast talk, which was the BBC Wales annual radio lecture of 1962, Saunders Lewis predicted that Welsh would cease to be a living language at the beginning of the twenty-first century if present trends continued.

'At long last the policy set out in the Act of Union of Wales and England in 1536 will have succeeded.'

He then quoted the report of Matthew Arnold, a school inspector, writing in 1855: 'It must always be the desire of a government to render its dominions, as far as possible, homogeneous. . . . Sooner or later the difference of language between Wales and England will probably be effaced . . . an event which is socially and politically so desirable.'

Saunders Lewis said that after 1536 the concept of Wales as a nation ceased to be a recollection, an ideal or a fact. And until the twentieth century there was no political attempt to restore the status of Welsh, or to have it recognized as an administrative language. 'If England and Wales are one completely united kingdom then the existence of Welsh is a reminder of a different condition, a danger to the union . . . the Act of Union cast Welsh out of the courts of rulers and the stately homes of the kingdom, out of the world of the leaders of society, where all learning, techniques, art and science were discussed.'

He then turned to the 'blue books' of 1847, the reports of inspectors who went to Wales to examine the education system, and quoted the report of one of them, Mr R. W. Lingen. 'My district exhibits the phenomenon of a peculiar language—isolating the mass from the upper portion of society; and as a further phenomenon it exhibits this mass engaged upon the most opposite occupations at points not very distant from each other; being, on the one side, rude and primitive agriculturists; on the other, smelters and miners, wantoning in plenty, and congregated in the densest accumulations. An incessant tide of immigration sets in from the former extreme to the latter. . . . Yet the families which are daily passing from one scene to the other do not thereby change their relative position in society. A new field is opened to them, but not a wider. They are never masters. . . . Whether in the country or among the furnaces, the Welsh element is never found at the top of the scale. . . . Equally in his new as in his old home, his language keeps him under the hatches, being one in which he can neither acquire nor communicate the necessary information. It is a language of old-fashioned agriculture, of theology and of simple rustic life, while all the world about him is English. He is left to live in an underworld of his own and the march of society goes . . . completely over his head.'

Saunders Lewis recalled that the reports of the inspectors were known in Wales as 'the betrayal of the blue books'. But, he said, the Lingen report's accuracy and astuteness were amazing. The report told the cruel truth and showed the inevitable fate of the language.

He commented: 'If it was the reaction against the blue books that gave rise to Welsh nationalism in the second half of the century it must also be admitted that the blue books were victorious. Despite the extreme anger and rage which they gave rise to, despite the fervent protests at their black depiction of Welsh nonconformity . . . the whole of Wales, and Welsh nonconformity in particular, adopted the entire policy and main recommendations of the disastrous report. The nation's leaders, laymen and ministers vigorously proceeded to establish a completely English system of education throughout Wales.'

Then he made an attack on the University of Wales. 'It is

responsible, more than any other institution, for the present inability of Welsh literature to give a complete portrayal of the life of a civilization. The policy of the University of Wales is the policy of the Act of Union . . . and the blue books; and Welsh Wales puts up with it.' He attacked, too, the anti-Welsh attitude of the established church in the nineteenth century.

Reviewing the position of the language in the twentieth century, he said: 'The tradition of political defence of the language is a tradition of suffering contempt and persecution. In Wales anything can be forgiven except being in earnest about the language. The language crisis now is a precarious situation. Welsh is a language in retreat in Wales, the language of a minority, and a minority still diminishing.'

He explored the change in government attitude to Welsh. 'The attitude has changed far more than any change there has been within Wales. Welsh is no longer considered to be a political offence. . . . It is now the Ministry of Education that encourages the Welsh people to become a bilingual nation, and so to gain the best of both worlds, the upper deck English world and the second class, not completely under the hatches, Welsh deck world. The vast majority of educational leaders in Wales see this as a magnanimous and worthy ideal. I personally am one of the so-called lunatic minority who see in it a respectable and easy death and tearless funeral of the Welsh language.

'One important lesson can be deduced from the government attitude. If Wales were to demand that Welsh be made an official language with English, the opposition would not come from the direction of the government or the Civil Service . . . the Civil Service has long since learned to accept revolutionary changes in the British Empire as part of the daily routine. It is from Wales, from local authorities and their officials, that the opposition would come, harshly, vindictively, fiercely.

'There is not the slightest chance of the Whitehall government ever adopting a Welsh standpoint. Persuasion, support, encouragement—all well and good. But to offend Carmarthen Council? Not on your life. The government will not lift a finger to save a minority which is so politically ineffective, pitifully helpless, so unable to defend itself, as is the Welsh minority in Wales.'

The broadcast ended with the controversial call for action: 'It is possible to save the Welsh language. Welsh Wales is still a substantial area of the land of Wales and the minority is not yet entirely insignificant.

'Go to it in earnest and without wavering, to make it impossible to conduct local authority or central government business without the Welsh language. Insist on the rate demand being either in Welsh or bilingual. Give notice to the Postmaster General that annual licences will not be paid unless they are available in Welsh. Demand that all summonses to appear in court be in Welsh. This is not a haphazard policy for isolated individuals. It would be essential to organize it and to proceed step by step, giving notice of intent and allowing time for the changes to be made. It is a policy for a movement and that movement should be active in those areas where Welsh is the everyday spoken language.

'Maybe you will say that this can never be achieved, that it is impossible to get sufficient Welshmen to agree and to organize such an important and energetic campaign. Perhaps you are right. All I maintain is that it is the only political question deserving of a Welshman's attention at the present time.

'I am aware of the difficulties. There would be stormy reactions from all quarters. The fines in the courts would be heavy and the consequences of not paying them would be costly, though not more costly than fighting purposeless parliamentary elections.

'I do not deny that there would be a period of hate and persecution and strife instead of the loving peacefulness so remarkable in Welsh political life today.

'To revive the Welsh language in Wales today is nothing less than a revolution. Success can only come through revolutionary methods. The language is more important than self-government. In my opinion, if we were to have any sort of self-government for Wales before the Welsh language is recognized and used as an official language in all the administration of state and local authority in the Welsh areas of the country, it would never attain official status and the doom of the language would come more quickly than it will come under English government.'

The word spread.

Saunders Lewis maintained that his lecture was intended to inspire *Plaid Cymru*, but the party, of course, could not commit itself to a policy of lawbreaking campaigning or civil disobedience. *Plaid Cymru* had many times stated that it could only work constitutionally.

(Eight years after the broadcast, MPs at the Welsh Grand Committee condemned Saunders Lewis for fostering a revolutionary attitude among sections of Welsh youth.)

In his lecture Saunders Lewis paid a tribute to a man and his wife who had for several years dug in their heels to get some recognition for the Welsh language. This couple, Mr and Mrs Trefor Beasley, started making a stand in 1952 when the rural district council of Llanelli, Carmarthenshire, a strongly Welsh area, sent them a rate demand. The Beasleys asked for a Welsh version and were refused. They then refused to pay rates until a Welsh form was forthcoming—and, during the next eight years they were summoned more than twelve times for non-payment of rates. Bailiffs went to their home three times and took furniture away to be sold to pay the rates. In terms of anxiety and inconvenience, let alone money, the Beasleys suffered considerably for their principle. But, at last, in 1960, the Llanelli council dismounted from its high horse, and sent the Beasleys what would have cost the council nothing in money or trouble in the first place, a bilingual rate form.

'The Beasleys' example shows how to go about it,' Saunders Lewis said.

At the *Plaid Cymru* summer school at Pontardulais in 1962 a group of students, mainly from University College, Aberystwyth, founded *Cymdeithas yr Iaith Gymraeg*—their badge, soon to be seen in jacket lapels throughout Wales, was a symbolic representation of a dragon's tongue.

In February of 1963 the society made its first public protest. A group of people, demanding that court summonses should be available in Welsh, blocked the bridge at Trefechan, Aberystwyth, by sitting down in the road. It was a rather ragged gesture, but it attracted attention as well as the inevitable contempt. The movement began to grow, the letters began to flow. More people started asking for Welsh summonses and for bilingual forms of all kinds.

The government sensed that the movement getting under way in Wales was not a flash in the pan. In 1963 it set up a committee, under the chairmanship of Sir David Hughes-Parry, to clarify the legal status of Welsh and consider whether changes should be made in the law. During the two years this committee sat the Welsh Language Society did not demonstrate. It concentrated instead on money raising and quiet campaigning. Several parents tried to register the births of their children in Welsh and some were fined when they refused to register in English.

Meanwhile the Council for Wales and Monmouthshire had been considering the language question and at the end of 1963 published the report *The Welsh Language Today*, one of the best surveys of the Welsh language ever compiled. The Council recommended that Welsh should have official status, that people should have the right to use it in courts, inquiries and tribunals, in local government, in election papers, in correspondence with government departments and in official documents.

The report had a sensitive regard for the emotional aspect of the language question. In its summary it said it had aimed at finding a policy on which the whole of Wales could unite. 'We are conscious of divisions in Wales on this question, but we are convinced that the majority of the people in Wales are anxious to see the Welsh language survive and flourish. . . . The survival and strength of a language depend on the exercise of the general will of the community. If the community do not favour the use of the language, government and other institutions can do little. Language cannot be imposed on a people: it must be embraced voluntarily. If the general attitude towards a language is one of apathy, the language will be lost. . . . An important first step is to ensure that there exists a right climate of opinion concerning the Welsh language. At present it is used by a substantial minority of the people in Wales. It is used in the home, in local communities and by various groups and societies. This use is a voluntary exercise of will, and as such must be respected in a democratic country. . . . This is the background against which official or individual decisions about the use of Welsh should be taken. While the language cannot be deliberately imposed upon people, neither should its use be thoughtlessly or deliberately undermined. . . . There are two guiding principles: firstly the firm protection of individual rights to use the language, and secondly, a positive and practical sympathy towards the aspirations of those who wish to see it survive and flourish. In this we take the view that those who do not speak the language have corresponding rights, and that these rights should be fully acknowledged.'

The Hughes-Parry committee reported in October 1965. It came out in favour of the principle of equal validity for Welsh and English. This meant that any form or document in Welsh would have the same validity in law as if it had been written in English. The committee decided against complete bilingualism, a disappointment to the Welsh Language Society. The principle of equal validity was approved by most of the Welsh Members of Parliament and was incorporated into the Welsh Language Act of 1967.

Most members of the language society regarded the Hughes-Parry report simply as a launching pad for a renewed campaign to secure the status of Welsh. There were demonstrations at Post Offices and police had to pull out the sit-down protesters who were asking for more bilingual forms. A number of people refused to pay motor car tax because application forms were available only in English. They refused to pay their fines and three went to prison. A few months later the Ministry of Transport announced it would make the forms available in Welsh. (There was a sequel to this part of the story in 1969. A campaign was started to secure bilingual motor tax discs. The Ministry said there was not room for two languages on the discs and put the matter out of its mind. Two hundred leading ministers of religion, teachers, professors and professional men signed a petition saying they would refuse to display tax discs on their cars and, if they were prosecuted, would not pay the fines. They also said they were concerned that the struggle for Welsh was being carried on mainly by young people. Quite soon the Ministry of Transport reviewed the situation and decided there was room for both languages on tax discs and began to print bilingual ones.)

The translators were being kept busy. The television licence,

G

the Highway Code, birth and marriage registers—more than 300 official forms and documents in common use—were printed in Welsh, or in bilingual form. The Post Office, regarded by many campaigners as a brick wall against which they banged heads, began to soften. The red vans were inscribed *Post Brenhinol* as well as Royal Mail. *Swddfa'r Post* inscriptions began to appear alongside Post Office. Banks voluntarily began to provide forms and cheque books in Welsh.

Although the activities of the language campaigners were causing a little discomfort to the authorities, they had not yet come to public notice in a big way. It was with the road signs campaign and the publicity achieved at the time of the investiture of Prince Charles that the language society made Welsh a public and political issue, polarized and divided opinion in Wales—and headed for a showdown with the authorities.

With tins and sprays of green paint, members of the society went about Wales daubing and spraying those road signs that carried only the English language versions of Welsh place-names.

Cardigan, for example, is in Welsh known as Aberteifi. Welsh speakers call Swansea Abertawe, Barmouth Abermo, Cardiff Caerdydd, Carmarthen Caerfyrddin, Holyhead Caergybi, Brecon Aberhonddhu, Fishguard Abergwaun. Scores of Welsh towns and villages have had their names anglicized. Here, then, was an opportunity for the Welsh Language Society to demonstrate in a non-violent, albeit illegal, fashion. The cause was bilingual road signs, but not just for their own sake. It was not a direct attack on English. The English-language road signs were a symbol of another language's superiority over theirs—that is what stuck in Welsh throats. If Welsh was to have equal validity with English, to have the official recognition in the spirit of the Welsh Language Act, bilingual road signs were, in the view of the society and many other people in Wales, indeed the majority, a matter of common justice.

'A Welsh child may grow up naturally with Welsh as his first language,' a minister of religion said to me, 'and then he begins to read and he sees on the road signs that the town he knows as Aberteifi has the different and official name of

Cardigan. He begins to believe that his language has second class status.'

Geraint Eckley, a teacher fined more than £40 for daubing road signs, and who went to prison for refusing to pay motor tax on the ground that the tax form was not (at the time) available in Welsh, said: 'I will go to prison again and again if need be. I am deeply committed to the struggle. The daubings of road signs shook people out of their apathy. Certainly we were at the receiving end of a lot of criticism, but the campaign was the opposite to hooliganism because its aim was to preserve, not destroy, something old and beautiful. And we have always accepted responsibility for what we did.

'If you ask why I do it, it is because the language is an essential, a central part, of my personality. It is the language that weaves my thoughts. It is closely associated with the best things in our national life. But the language is in an inferior position and that makes us feel inferior, too. So we do something about it.'

In 1968 the Welsh Language Society had elected as its chairman a student of architecture called Dafydd Iwan Jones. The son of a Congregational minister, he was at this time just establishing himself as a folk singer and had shortened his name to Dafydd Iwan. He graduated in architecture but never went into an office because he found he could earn his living through concerts, television appearances and records, singing his own songs in the Welsh language. He played guitar adequately and his songs, which were about love and about Wales, were very much in tune with the burgeoning concern that young people were feeling about their language and their country.

They had the right edge of sadness and passion about them. They were patriotic songs. And one of the best known was the first one he composed which was about Wales and the old warriors and the threat to the culture. Its message for young people was 'It's up to us now'.

It was not long before Dafydd Iwan became well known, and admired, as a language campaigner and as a singer of songs that caught a mood. It was not long, either, before he became, as far as a considerable section of the Welsh public was concerned, one of the most disliked men in Wales. For he and his society announced their disapproval of the investiture of Prince Charles at Caernarvon.

Young people began to wear tin lapel badges saying '*Dim Sais yn Dywysog Cymru*'—'No Englishman for Prince of Wales.' Dafydd Iwan wrote and recorded a song which was a satire on the prince and the investiture. It was called *Carlo*—a Welsh pet-name for Charles—and it became a best seller. It was mis-understood to be a vulgar personal attack on the prince.

Abusive letters started arriving at Dafydd Iwan's home and a newspaper, urging its readers not to buy the record *Carlo*, described the singer as 'the man who has brought shame on every Welshman'. Not surprisingly, this attack was welcomed by some. Much of Wales was looking forward to the investiture, to the fun, the prestige, the recognition. As it prepared to wallow in the limelight, it did not like the idea of the great occasion being criticized or smeared by a handful of people who, in their view, were stupid young men, hairy hooligans, fanatics, extremists and bloody nationalists. ('What on earth will other people think of us?')

'I had misgivings about opposing the investiture, but we had no choice. You cannot let things go simply because it is tactically better to do so,' Dafydd Iwan said. 'Public opinion was inflamed against us because of the public relations effort from the other side. The investiture symbolized what we are fighting against . . . Wales could be recognized as an interesting, quaint and colourful extension of England and there was lip service to the Welsh language. This was worse than being ignored altogether. It was a cleverly thought-out political stunt. Nationalist opponents to the scheme would just look churls and spoil-sports. It was a gimmick and the person I felt sympathy for was Prince Charles—for being used to prop up the image of a vanishing empire.'

At Cilmeri, near Builth Wells, in Breconshire, there is a monument marking the place where Llewelyn, the last native Prince of Wales, was hacked to death by an Englishman in 1282. Four days before the investiture more than a thousand people attended a rally at the stone; it was organized by the language society as a protest against 'the insult of investing an Englishman as Prince of Wales'.

Dafydd Iwan said then that the road signs campaign would be stepped up. It was. To this day there are hundreds of signs throughout Wales defaced with green paint or plastered with stickers saying '*Cymraeg!*'—'Welsh!' But at the end of 1969 the language society announced that it would cause no more damage for a year to enable local authorities to reconsider the requests for bilingual road signs and to announce a firm policy of providing such signs. The reaction in many local authority offices to this announcement can be imagined. Mr George Thomas, the Labour Government Secretary of State for Wales, and other Members of Parliament, had already said that bilingual signs would be too expensive, confusing and dangerous.

Nevertheless, Cardiganshire and Merioneth wanted to bring in bilingual signs and the Secretary of State, conceding very little, eventually gave permission for signs in a limited category, like place-names, to be bilingual. But directional signs were to stay in English.

It was becoming clear that the Welsh Language Society was not to be dismissed simply as a band of extremist hooligans. It was small, it had fewer than 2000 members, yet it was clearly the tip of an iceberg, the manifestation of a deep-seated concern. Even if they disapproved of the young people's methods, a considerable number of people of standing and influence, teachers, professors, lecturers, ministers and professional men, supported the society's aims. In the campaigning of 1969–71 the society was never out of the news for long. There was a pattern of court cases, imprisonments, demonstrations, occupation of courts and BBC buildings.

The effect of all this was to make more people think about the issue and to harden opinion one way or the other. It has always been acceptable in many circles to support the aims, but not the activities, of the language society, but as the campaign has gone on more people have been drawn to approving the methods.

In January of 1970 Dafydd Iwan was arrested and imprisoned for refusing to pay a fine and costs of £56 imposed for daubing road signs during the society's campaign. Then, in an amazing and unprecedented gesture, twenty-one Welsh magistrates contributed to a fund to pay his fine and secure his release. The originator of this move, Mr E. D. Jones, the former national librarian of Wales, wrote from his home in Aberystwyth to forty magistrates. He said in his letter that a chasm had opened between the older and younger generations in Wales and that the imprisonment of Dafydd Iwan would make the gap more difficult to bridge. The twenty-one magistrates who sent money paid between £1 and £5 each. One of them, Mr Emlyn Vaughan Griffiths, a farmer, said: 'I feel there is a difference between a criminal act and an act of conscience.'

There was another surprise to come. Dr Glyn Simon, then Archbishop of Wales, went to see Dafydd Iwan in prison and told him of the magistrates' gesture.

The whole business was naturally controversial. The *Western Mail* ruled that the magistrates had placed themselves in a contradictory position because Dafydd Iwan had been fined for criminal acts and their duty was to further respect for the law.

It was not the first time that the language campaigners had touched the consciences of magistrates. At most of their court appearances, members of the language society sang the Welsh national anthem—presenting those in court with a dilemma. For the anthem has a sacred place in the hearts of many Welsh people. So some magistrates have found themselves standing to attention, occasionally joining in, while the people they have just fined have sung the anthem.

Two days before Dafydd Iwan's release, a group from the language society shattered the peace of a libel case in the High Court in London. They burst into the courtroom, singing and handing out leaflets, calling for the release of their society's chairman and demanding justice for the Welsh language. For this contempt of his court the judge gave out sentences of three months' imprisonment to those who would not apologize.

On his release from prison, having served three weeks of his three months' sentence, Dafydd Iwan said: 'We are not anarchists. We do not like breaking the law, but we have no choice.'

In October 1970, at its annual meeting in Aberystwyth, the society agreed to step up its campaign. It was agreed that small posters should be stuck on English language road signs, warning the authorities that members of the society would uproot them in view of the continuing inaction by the government on the question of bilingual signs. Soon, the road signs were toppling all over Wales. More than £6000 worth were pulled down. One man, climbing up a tall sign to get better leverage for his spanner, fell and broke his leg.

Increasingly, the older generation in the Welsh-speaking community were feeling involved in the struggle. There was a kind of anguish among the middle-aged. In 1971 a petition signed by 5000 people, largely ministers, lecturers, professors and other 'respectable' citizens, urged the Secretary of State to take action to get local authorities to provide bilingual signs. A deputation of leading Welshmen went to see the Secretary of State at the Welsh Office and, shortly afterwards, it was announced that the government was setting up a committee to examine the issue of bilingual signs.

Meanwhile, the activities of the language campaigners were causing increasing concern in some quarters. The Director of Public Prosecutions ordered the arrest of eight members of the Welsh Language Society for conspiring to remove and destroy road signs. Conspiracy is a serious charge, has to be heard at a court of assize and merits a heavier sentence than magistrates can impose.

When the eight men appeared at Aberystwyth magistrates' court, to be sent for trial, there was a noisy demonstration and sixty people were carried out of the court. Outside a large crowd watched as some forty road signs were hurled onto the court steps. A few weeks later, when the accused men were making applications at Carmarthen Assizes, fifty-one people were held for singing in the court and were imprisoned for contempt.

Just before the trial at Swansea, Dafydd Iwan said to me: 'Direct action and demonstration does not come naturally to me. It has been a long and intellectual process that has convinced me of the importance of the struggle and that this kind of action is necessary. I am convinced that had the Welsh Language Society not acted, the language would not be as healthy as it is now. Not that its situation is particularly healthy.

'I see this struggle as part of the worldwide movement in

which small countries and cultures, minorities of all kinds, are fighting to retain their identity against uniformity, mass culture and the big power blocs. This is, in effect, a civil rights movement and we identify with all those small groups battling against the tide.

'Welsh has always been an important part of my life. My father is a minister and I was brought up in Carmarthenshire in the traditional mould: everything revolved around the chapel, the home and the *eisteddfod*. The only activity that was not connected with Welsh was the pictures. As a child I never associated English with the idea of a threat to my natural language. But the eleven-plus in Carmarthenshire, in those days, could be taken in English or in Welsh and I was the only one in my class who took it in Welsh. That was the first thing that struck me as being rather odd. But to me and my parents there was no choice because Welsh was my first language, although my mother had been an English teacher and had ensured that my English was fluent.

'At grammar school the atmosphere changed completely. English was the main language, the language of instruction. My parents were nationalists, and very keen ones, but I do not remember them stressing the matter of language. After all, there was enough going on in our home and community to keep Welsh in the ascendancy. It was only after I left school that I realized that the anglicizing effect of secondary schools has had—is having—a dramatic influence in Wales.

'I went to University College, Aberystwyth, to study architecture. At that time the founders of the Welsh Language Society were there and gradually I became involved in the language question. I joined the society in 1963. The great row about the Tryweryn dam had a strong effect on me. It shook the whole national movement and I was particularly affected by the symbolism of the blowing up of a pylon near the dam site. It was a blow for Wales. As the language campaign progressed I became involved in demonstrations. My first court appearance was during the agitating for bilingual tax discs for cars—I was picked up for not having a disc. The fine was paid anonymously. There were more court appearances and finally I was sent to prison.

92

'All this activity is making people think about the language. They may think what they like about us, as long as they think about the language. Today, non-violent campaigning which is difficult to squash is the only positive way to get something done. Official status, on its own, will not save Welsh, but it makes an important contribution.

'I can see the language society growing into something much more than a protest movement. If it is to be taken more seriously it should be associated with the Welsh-speaking areas. It is common sense to concentrate our efforts on Welsh Wales where the big threat to the Welsh-speaking society is depopulation, the lack of work and the influx of people from England buying up holiday homes and retirement cottages. The language must be valid; I don't want it kept in a glass case; there's no future for the language without a vigorous society to speak it.

'Probably the odds are against what we talk about as our goal —a Wales where everybody can speak Welsh. It must be a long way off, I suppose. But it is not something to be optimistic or pessimistic about. There is nothing else for it but to go on fighting. The people who are campaigning for the language are doomed to be possessed by the struggle. They cannot switch off their commitment because it is a part of their personality and driving force.

'The language society is a movement made up largely of young people, mostly well-educated and interested in the values of life, and we are getting a lot of support. This, after all, is a time to act. It is not a time to write, to compose sad poems. The poets are often unaware of the political situation and by not acting they are escaping their responsibilities.

'When I started singing I sang songs in English simply because there were no songs written for the guitar in Welsh. Then I began to compose in Welsh and there was no need to sing in English. As time has gone by, it has become increasingly important for me to stick to singing in Welsh. It is part of the message. I have written about eighty songs and made more than a dozen records. People credit me with starting Welsh pop, but I didn't. I write love songs and patriotic songs and they simply reflect a mood among a section of the young people of Wales. Members of Parliament, and others, are quick to

93

dismiss the songs as a lot of nationalist propaganda, but they are patriotic songs rather than political ones, and if they have a rather serious tone that is because of the situation. To write a happy song about the Welsh condition is asking too much.'

Dafydd Iwan was one of the eight members of the language society arraigned before Mr Justice Mars-Jones, a Welsh-speaking judge, at Swansea, in May 1971. The judge ruled that every word spoken in Welsh would be translated into English, and vice versa. The accused spoke only in Welsh and the judge was meticulous in his insistence that every word said in the court should be translated. Even the small asides and 'Silence in court!' were translated from one language into the other. 'That Dafydd Iwan—he can speak English better than most Englishmen,' said a spectator, bringing up the old grumble. 'It's just bloody-mindedness. I could kick the stuffing out of him!'

The eight made it clear from the outset that they regarded the trial as a political one. Two of them, Gwilym Tudur, a bookseller, and Frederick Francis, who had de-anglicized his name to Ffred Ffransis, said they did not recognize the court and refused to take part in the proceedings. Apart from those formal occasions when it was necessary for them to be in the dock, they spent the trial in the cells. The proceedings lasted ten days and were punctuated by shouts and demonstrations by people in the court. Fifteen were arrested and imprisoned for contempt. A small crowd holding banners and placards kept vigil outside in a show of support for the accused. Twice, young people broke through the strong police cordon and threw themselves in front of the judge's car as it left the court.

Halfway through the trial, on a Saturday, a crowd of people gathered in Swansea to demonstrate their support for the language society leaders on trial, to walk through the city and to sign a statement of collective responsibility for the removal of monolingual road signs. Police moved in to break up the demonstration and forty-three men and women were arrested for obstruction and were later fined. One of them, Mr Ned Thomas, a university lecturer and editor of the English language cultural magazine *Planet*, said to the magistrates: 'On my return to Wales after fifteen years away I was appalled at the situation, at the way in which elementary cultural rights which exist for smaller minorities in civilized countries are, in Wales, the subject of slow, grudging, forced concession.

'I was also appalled to see how any serious effort on behalf of the language was misrepresented by Welsh Members of Parliament as a political, nationalist act, and the way in which some of the people in authority exploited the division between English-speakers and Welsh-speakers, suggesting that the former were in some way threatened by the latter. This is patently untrue. The public presence of Welsh alongside English threatens nobody. . . . The drift towards conflict springs from an injustice caused not by malice but by lack of imagination and courage, and by inflexibility among politicians and administrators.

'I realize that the Welsh language movement is easily made to seem a movement of cranks or political fanatics who can speak English if they try. But if you lived in Cardiganshire, where I do, or in any part of Welsh-speaking Wales, you would realize that this is the everyday language of thousands of people . . . I am convinced that more has been done for the Welsh language as a result of the Welsh Language Society's illegal campaigns than would otherwise have been done. I have been struck by their concern with non-violence and by their success in drawing non-Welsh-speakers and, indeed, non-Welshmen, to their cause.'

The evidence in the conspiracy trial was straightforward enough and there was little dispute with the facts. One of the accused was acquitted and, at the end, the seven remaining were convicted and then addressed the court at great length. Gwilym Tudur, a veteran of the language campaign, said: 'We are not criminals secretly conspiring, but workmen rolling up our sleeves in the winter to cut a furrow towards the spring. And if you call us extremists the name is a tribute. Our country is experiencing a national crisis as we see our unique civilization slipping towards oblivion. I will continue my part in the battle as before . . . it is sweet to be a Welshman.'

The judge gave sentences of twelve months to five of the men and of six months and three months to the others. The terms were suspended for three years. The judge said: 'I believe you

95

are committed to a dangerous course of self-destruction and I want to give you the last chance to pause and think before you plunge into the abyss. There is no doubt that each of you has some fine qualities and none of you lacks courage. You are prepared to make sacrifices for what you believe, and one or two of you show the highest quality of all, a basic humility. But I have been shocked at the display of blind intolerance, intellectual and spiritual arrogance, the studied insolence and the black hatred that has been displayed by some of you in this trial.'

Blinking in the sunshine, the leaders of the language society came out to meet their supporters. Under an enormous Red Dragon, a minister of religion said, with a barely contained excitement: 'This is just the beginning.'

(Three months later there was a piquant scene at the national *eisteddfod* at Bangor. Dafydd Iwan was admitted with due ceremony to the bardic circle and among those robed bards who stood watching the ritual of welcome was Mr Justice Mars-Jones.)

The trial, and the setting up by the Secretary of State of a committee to investigate the question of bilingual signs, were peaks in the language campaign. In the meantime the ground had been prepared for an altogether more difficult battle. For some years, concern about the effect of television and radio on the Welsh language had been spreading and hardening. The feeling developed that unless there was a good deal more Welsh on the screens and on the radios the language would suffer increasingly severe damage.

The Welsh Language Society submitted to the BBC and the ITA a document calling for an independent broadcasting corporation for Wales to run a television channel of Welsh language programmes, a channel of English language programmes for Wales, and a similar service on radio. These services, it was proposed, would be financed through licence revenue, advertisements and government subsidy.

'The present broadcasting policy for Wales (which is decided in London) is a form of culture imperialism against our country,' said the society's document. 'Radio and television are being used to force another civilization on our nation and to condition our people to think as Englishmen. The broadcasting media are being used to dispossess the people of Wales of their national heritage and to kill the values of the Welsh society. . . . The few Welsh programmes cannot do more than emphasize the idea that Wales is a small, insignificant province of England. . . . The children of Wales are at the mercy of all the anglicizing influences despite the efforts of parents to keep homes Welsh in language. In 1963 the Council of Wales, on the Welsh language, said: "The attention given to the children of Wales on television is painfully inadequate."

'Where the broadcasting media—like education—could be used to ensure that all the children of Wales maintain their grasp on their national heritage, they are being used to kill the Welsh language on their lips and to lessen their loyalty to their country.'

The Broadcasting Council for Wales replied in April 1971 that the setting up of the kind of service envisaged by the Welsh Language Society would cost more than the combined resources available to the BBC and the ITA in Wales. It could be financed only by a large increase in licence fees and advertising revenue, or by a large government subsidy. The council added that it had no evidence of widespread demand for changes in the present system and it reminded the society that the operating expenditure for Wales, as far as the BBC was concerned, was nearly as large as that for Scotland or the North, although licence revenue in Scotland was twice as large as for Wales and in the North was five times as great.*

The language society was in no mood to take this No for an answer. 'We are not asking for the moon,' wrote one, in a magazine article. 'We are asking for our own radio and television channels. We are tired of being fobbed off with excuses. . . . Let the producers of cultural conformity and mass mediocrity beware. This issue is dynamite—for on it rests the life and death of a people. Faced with death people become desperate.'

* In February 1972 the Broadcasting Council put the cost of setting up a basic radio and TV service for Wales at £6·86 million, and £3·6 million a year to run: the cost of an all embracing service would be £38 million and the running cost £19 million a year.

A few people by this time had been in court for refusing to pay their television licence fees as part of the campaign for a better deal for Welsh broadcasting. And in the weekly newspaper *Baner ac Amserau Cymru* the idea of a large-scale refusal to pay the licence fee was mooted. Support for this grew and within a few weeks several hundred people had their names published under a statement saying they would refuse to pay their fee from the autumn of 1971 and would instead put the money into a fund to support a Welsh broadcasting service.

And in July, at three o'clock one morning, ten members of the language society climbed five television transmitters and roped themselves about a hundred feet off the ground. They said their object was to stop the transmitters putting out programmes, but in this they failed. The larger purpose of the demonstration, however—the publicity—was achieved. It was the beginning of a new phase in the fight for the language.

Meanwhile, the Bowen committee investigating the question of bilingual road signs was told by *Plaid Cymru*: 'The demand for bilingual signs is based upon the status of the Welsh language in the community.

'One is forced to ask the basic question: is Welsh an alien language? If the committee is of this opinion it is unreasonable for us to expect it to advocate the provision of bilingual signs. To concede on the other hand that Welsh is a British language makes the language very much the concern of the British government. The patronage of the government is extended unstintingly to English and until such time as the same patronage is extended to Welsh the accusation, frequently made, that it is the British government which is responsible for killing the latter will continue to have considerable force.

'It is generally recognized now in the field of socio-linguistics that the overriding factor affecting the spread or retreat of language is the political one. N. Glazer, in *The Process and Problems of Language Maintenance, An Integrative Review*, wrote: "One can hardly overestimate the importance of some official status in maintaining a language. It gives it social status among its native users and serves in part as a barrier against self-deprecation and embarrassment. A little of state support in the form of official printing presses, court proceedings and school use can at times do more to establish a language than a vast amount of energetic activity by language loyalists."

'A great deal of state support for Welsh could transform the linguistic situation in Wales. An acceptance of the principle of bilingual signs would be a pledge of governmental good will— a small thing in itself but a gesture of deep psychological significance.'

Glamorgan County Council's evidence to the committee took a sharply different tone. The county surveyor said: 'Road signs are already an incursion on amenity. They are big and ugly. Bilingualism would make them bigger and uglier. When a sign is bilingual it loses clarity and becomes a source of danger. I think bilingual signing abroad is done at the expense of safety.'

Cardiganshire gave its support for two-language signs and declared: 'We find it difficult to believe that the authorities in Switzerland, Holland, Belgium, Ireland, Finland, South Africa and Canada would permit a system of sign posting which holds a threat to the safety of people on their roads. We believe there is a fund of goodwill towards the Welsh language and a willingness to ensure its survival. The greatest obstacles are psychological: a tendency to magnify the importance of known difficulties and to imagine difficulties where none exists.'

In a lecture to the British Association at Swansea in September, Mr Dewi Watkin Powell, a barrister (now a Crown Court judge), said that the disorder taking place in Wales on the language issue could be blamed on the reluctance of government, national and local, to give Welsh equal status with English. The time had come, he said, for the authorities to look at the Welsh Language Act of 1967 and ask themselves what they could do to implement its spirit and intentions. Society could not tolerate interference with the running of its courts, but 'when both the protagonists of the language, and those charged with prosecuting and punishing them when they break the law, purport, not without justification, to be upholding law and order, it is time to consider where the conflict originates and how it can be resolved'.

By this time seventeen members of the language society had been charged with conspiring to interfere with television transmissions. This followed the demonstrations involving five

99

transmitters in July. Three were also charged with breaking into the Granada television centre in Manchester and breaking equipment worth more than £800. The preliminary hearing, at Mold magistrates' court, in Flintshire, collapsed in uproar after the defendants' request that the case be heard in Welsh was rejected. Four interpreters were called, to translate English proceedings into Welsh, but refused to take part in the case 'as a matter of principle and conscience'. Their action was greeted with prolonged applause from the public in the gallery. Then public and accused men joined in strident singing. The prosecution was forced to get a bill of indictment from the High Court to have the men sent for trial.

When, in October, the case came up at Flintshire Assizes, it was the focus of endless demonstrations—and more fuel was piled on to the controversy over the use of Welsh in the courts. The day the trial started, a letter appeared in *The Times*, signed by the Archbishop of Wales and thirteen other Welshmen. It was called a 'declaration of rights' and said: 'We hold that to compel Welsh-speaking defendants to submit to trial in English, against their will, before law courts in Wales, is a violation of the rights of man. . . . In the name of justice we demand that any laws that violate the principle of equal linguistic rights in Wales be repealed—so that Welsh-speaking Welshmen shall not be treated in their own country as though they were aliens speaking a foreign tongue.'

Three of the defendants refused to take part in the trial and were kept in the cells. They maintained they had a right to a trial in their own language in their own country.

The men who had smashed equipment at the Granada centre —they had sat in the studio drinking coffee while waiting to be found and arrested—were sent to prison. Ffred Ffransis, long term and zealous language campaigner, who had been given a suspended sentence at the Swansea trial in May, went to prison for two years and his two colleagues were imprisoned for a year. Of the television mast demonstrators, Gronw Davies, who had taken over the chairmanship of the language society, was sentenced to six months and ten others received suspended sentences.

In a number of ways the language struggle hardened in 1971.

As views polarized there was an increasing resentment and condemnation of the militant language campaigners from some quarters. In this sensitive situation many people began to wonder whether there was now a genuine danger of a harmful division developing in Welsh society.

# 6 *Cofia Dryweryn*

Capel Celyn was a small village in the quiet Tryweryn valley in the hill country between Bala and Ffestiniog in North Wales. In and around it lived about seventy people and the community was steeped in the Welsh tradition. The people earned their merely modest living through farming, and their social life, with its strong cultural stream and chapel base, followed an old and rich pattern. The village was in the Penllyn district, the home of *penillion*, which is the singing of verses to the accompaniment of the harp, and there were many harps in the valley. People met for hour upon hour of singing, poetry, reading and the special verse-arts of the Welsh language. Indeed, Capel Celyn, although an obscure settlement, was a precious and largely unspoiled nugget of Welsh values. Today, however, the name of the valley, Tryweryn, is, for many people in Wales, a shorthand expression for a whole chapter of emotions, and the word is painted on walls and bridges up and down Wales. So is the slogan *Cofia Dryweryn*—Remember Tryweryn. For the corporation of Liverpool, with measured arrogance, and without consulting anyone involved, announced that it would have the valley as a reservoir and proceeded to do just that. The harps have vanished, for Capel Celyn no longer exists; farms, school, chapel, store, cottages, are at the bottom of a silent lake.

The episode of Tryweryn was a traumatic one and it is one of the keys to what has been happening in Wales in recent years. From it sprang a great anger and a hardening of resolve; for many men and women it was an awakening, the first indication that the values of Wales were in danger and were meaningless to the authorities in England; it started people thinking and, for a small group of men, it was the last straw that made them channel rage into a cold determination to strike blows for Wales with stolen gelignite and time switches. The bomb attacks on water pipelines and government offices went on for more than four years, but the reverberations of Tryweryn are being felt still. 'Tryweryn', wrote Gwynfor Evans, the Welsh Nationalist

Party leader, 'will become a word of fateful significance for
Wales. It may become as well known as a verb as Quisling has
become as a noun.'

The drowning of valleys in Wales is a sensitive and
emotional subject. The lost battle for Tryweryn was fought for
much the same kind of cause as the lost battle for Penyberth in
Caernarvonshire in 1936, which is described in Chapter 5. To
many Welshmen Tryweryn was, and is, a scandal of the first
order, although some people in Wales and certainly the corporation of Liverpool and the government did not see it that
way at all. It was simply that Liverpool, a major city, needed
water for its factories and its population of more than 600,000.
These needs had to be balanced against the uprooting of a tiny
village of a few dozen people in a sleepy corner of upland
Wales.

It was quite obvious what course had to be taken, a regret-
table course, but a fact of life in a modern industrial and thirsty
society. It was expected that the noise of complaint would be
softened by compensation money, the noise of protest from
Wales could be explained as the work of troublemakers, and, in
any case, once the legal business was tied up and the people
moved out, the fuss would die away.

It did not work out like that, for the people in Wales saw the
matter as one of important principle. With the Welsh tradition
being everywhere eroded by economic forces and depopulation,
such a culturally rich, Welsh-speaking community was of
immense value, something that, however small, Wales could not
afford to lose. And Liverpool's scheme would make it a total
loss. People were appalled to see just how vulnerable Wales was:
they had expected or hoped that English authorities would
consider the social aspects, would take care where they trod.
Liverpool was portrayed as a bully shrugging off protests to
grab a piece of land. A defence committee was formed and 125
local authorities, with trade union branches and religious and
cultural organizations, gave their support, passing resolutions
condemning the scheme. A majority of the Welsh Members of
Parliament came out against Liverpool (twenty-seven of the
thirty-six members voted against the Bill promoting the scheme
at the second reading, and none voted for it). Not everyone in

103

Wales was against, but, far from there being just a few trouble-makers, it was clear that there was a large measure of united and responsible opposition to the reservoir. Indeed, Wales was united on a simple issue as never before.

Liverpool, with an attitude of pain, now indicated that the Welsh people were prepared to allow 600,000 people to go thirsty. But this was a deception. The city was getting all it needed for domestic purposes, and more, from another Welsh valley reservoir, Lake Vyrnwy. Tryweryn water was not wanted for the children and the teapots. It was wanted for industrial expansion and for re-sale at a profit. The profit motive intensified the anger within Wales.

Liverpool had earmarked Tryweryn without consulting the people, the local council of Merioneth County Council; nor would it receive a deputation. Gwynfor Evans went to Liverpool and tried to address the members of the council, but he found himself shouting against an uproar and a banging of desks, and was eventually carried out by the police. Subsequently the people of Capel Celyn marched through Liverpool's streets and Gwynfor Evans was invited to speak to the council, this time in peace. Later, when the matter was put to the vote, 90 of the 160 councillors voted for the drowning of Tryweryn. A Labour councillor who voted against was expelled from his party. A national conference, called by the Lord Mayor of Cardiff, prepared an alternative reservoir scheme in the Tryweryn valley which would have spared the village. But it would have been more expensive. Liverpool refused to receive the representation of the conference to discuss the matter.

In Parliament, in July 1957, at the third reading of Liverpool's Bill, promoters and opponents came to an arrangement not to debate the issue and the Bill went through in a few minutes. Then it was passed by the House of Lords. 'There can be no question that emotions in Wales have been aroused,' said Mr Geoffrey Lawrence, who put Liverpool's case in the Lords, 'but Liverpool corporation have to take the constitution as they find it. There is no separate Welsh government. There is no separate demarcation of Wales from England from the point of view of water supplies.' There was to be no more singing in Capel Celyn. And in Welsh Wales, certainly, there were few men less popular than Mr Henry Brooke, then Minister for Welsh Affairs. He knew something of Welsh values but in the view of the Save Tryweryn movement he had worked only to help Liverpool. They remembered this part of one of his speeches in the Commons: 'Water shortages might occur in the next few years on Merseyside and in south-west Lancashire. I cannot believe that preservation of the Welsh way of life requires us to go as far as that. I cannot believe that the Welsh people, of all people, want to stand outside the brotherhood of man to that extent.'

Mr Brooke was asked not to attend the National *Eisteddfod* of Wales, the only person ever to receive such a request. It was the ultimate gesture of Welsh disdain.

Many people have said to me that Tryweryn was for them a shock and a kind of landmark. It indicated that Wales had no power to create its own conditions, or to secure its particular possessions. People felt they had been treated with contempt, and, indeed, the *Western Mail* stiffly remarked: 'There has been every appearance of complete contempt for Welsh opinion on the part both of the Liverpool corporation and of Parliament.'

The episode had two effects on the nationalist party. In the short term it threatened to tear it in two. Out of the anger and the resentment of defeat there grew an emotional move among some nationalists to retaliate with dramatic gestures and the talk was of using 'non-constitutional' methods, by which they presumably meant putting dynamite under some important piece of public property. The split of opinion was very serious for a time, but the moderate view prevailed as anger cooled. The leaders of *Plaid Cymru* were determined that the party should remain a political one and knew that, had the people who were for physical force had their way, the party would have been broken. There was no immediate effect on the strength of the party after Tryweryn, no rush to join the nationalist ranks, but, as the ripples spread, *Plaid Cymru*'s strength grew. In the long term, Tryweryn, which crystallized the Welsh situation socially and politically for many people, put more bone into the nationalist movement.

Although tempers gradually grew calmer within the nationalist party a few young Welshmen still burned with the idea of hitting back. In September 1962 two men opened the top of an oil tank on the Tryweryn dam site and released 1000 gallons. In the small hours of 10 February 1963, a transformer supplying electricity to the site was blown up and a university student was subsequently imprisoned for causing the explosion. Shortly afterwards, an attempt was made to blow up a pylon carrying power cables to the dam site.

In October 1963 the Tryweryn dam and reservoir, which cost £3,700,000, was opened by the Lord Mayor of Liverpool. It was not a happy occasion. There was stone throwing, shouting and fireworks. But there was a little amusement for the Welsh people there. The sound of Welsh voices, lifted in song, drifted in the air. It sounded rather like a hymn and the Lord Mayor and the councillors and corporation officials listened in respectful silence. It was indeed an old hymn tune and the words were repeated over and over by a group of youths. . . .

'Twll dîn pob Sais. . . .'

Which, being translated, is 'Arseholes to all Englishmen'.

Although the battle for Tryweryn was lost it ensured that in the future a cynical take-over of land across the Welsh border, with scant regard for people, would never be so easy. The next major reservoir scheme, in the Clywedog Valley, near Llanidloes, Montgomeryshire, did not drown a village, although a few farmers lost their homes, and the county authority was given seats on the management body. Still, work on the dam was disrupted by a bomb blast which did £30,000 worth of damage.

The public inquiry in 1970 into the Severn River Authority's intention to drown the Dulas valley, south of Llanidloes, was a milestone. Here, for the first time, the worth of a living community, the intangible qualities of community life were considered and valued. The inspector who conducted the inquiry noted that the valley's defence committee based their case on the assurance given in 1966 by Mr Cledwyn Hughes, the first Secretary of State for Wales in the Labour Government, that he would not agree to the development of sites which involved the drowning of villages, the disruption of whole communities or the use of first class land. No one wanted to deprive Englishmen of water, but here was a valley community of about 300 people, which was, according to evidence given at the inquiry,

'an intricate network of community relations . . . with strong
family links . . . a most neighbourly community with an
unusually strong religious and cultural life. The Dulas community is vigorous and lively and leads a satisfying and enviable
existence beyond the reach of urbanization. Young people
remain to follow on their parents and set an example of how
rural mid-Wales can resuscitate itself. The community has a
right to life, liberty and the pursuit of happiness. To destroy
such a community would be an act of vandalism.'

The people of the Dulas valley won the day: the inspector, in
his report, said: 'I conclude that the case . . . has not been
justified against all alternatives and that, because of the consequences for agriculture and particularly for the community,
the use of the Dulas valley for the next regulating reservoir in
the Severn would not be authorized.' The Secretary of State
could hardly over-rule that recommendation in spite of the
pressures upon him in view of the concern about water supplies
in the country as a whole and in the Midlands in particular. It
was another indication of the value to Wales of a Cabinet
minister responsible for Welsh affairs.

The Dulas decision was naturally welcomed throughout
Wales and people wondered why the authorities had been so
stubborn in the past, why community considerations had not
been thought important at the time of Tryweryn. The decision
was especially welcomed in another valley, fifty miles to the
south, the Senni valley in Breconshire. This was the setting of a
long-standing battle. The Usk River Authority needed another
reservoir urgently and was anxious to investigate the Senni.
But the valley people rigged up an air-raid siren in a holly tree
and kept a sharp lookout for strangers. Whenever surveyors
drove into the valley the siren was sounded and the people
blocked the roads with tractors or just sat down and refused to
admit the 'enemy'. After more than a year of this the river
authority announced retreat and the renewed search for other,
less contentious, sites.

The sparing of Dulas, although a milestone, is by no means
the end of the water problem. Rather, it is the beginning of a
new chapter. The demand for water in Britain is expected to
double by the end of this century and beautiful mid-Wales,

with its rain and rivers, cannot escape its role as a water store. The surveyors will be out on the mountains and the geologists will be examining the sample cores; more valleys must be drowned. There is plenty of water available: Wales uses about 150 million gallons a day at present, but it has been estimated that there is in Wales an untapped surplus amounting to 800 million gallons a day.

The nationalist party takes the view that water in Wales should be regarded, like oil in other countries, as a natural resource—the major resource of its poorest region—and that a Welsh water development authority should be set up to exploit it, to site the reservoirs and bargain with other authorities to secure royalties for water sales. In this way damage to communities would be largely avoided and, with water 'a price-conscious commodity', there would be money to aid the development of rural areas, much more than the users now pay in rates for their water. From England, not to say some parts of Wales, this may appear a narrow-minded idea based in chauvinism. But Welsh people do not object that their water goes to England; they object to the manner in which it is done. In the past they have had genuine cause for grievance. The reservoir hunters have not always been as open as they might. They have been arrogant and inconsiderate and have nearly always followed the criterion that the best water is the cheapest water; they have failed to think about people. That they now have to think seriously about the community aspects of their scheme is, perhaps, the most positive gain for Wales which emerged from the lost battle of Tryweryn.*

* In a reorganization of water resources administration in Britain, a Welsh national water development authority is to be established. It is hoped that this will take some of the heat out of the 'water issue'.

# 7 'Past Llewelyn's grave'

'Which is the way to the Abbey Cwmhir?'
'Llewelyn rest in peace.'
'Which is the way to Builth Wells?'
'Past Llewelyn's grave.'
There was a recent time in Wales when these phrases were
the challenges and passwords which would admit a man to a
ride on a cloud: to a strange brotherhood which throve on
dreams and fantasies and beer-built schemes, which puffed
itself up with hot air, and all manner of swaggering and postur-
ing and boastful talk, made exaggeration a kind of life-style,
flirted haphazardly with danger and grew surrealistically
larger than life. Eventually the authorities took it to a court of
assize and gave it such a thorough shaking and throttling that
nothing was left at all but a faint air of disillusion and the
uncomfortable feeling that those involved in its life and long
trial were part of a charade. The name of this brotherhood,
which comprised no more than three dozen fully paid-up
romancers, was the Free Wales Army.

This was a group of tap-room soldiers, to whom a round
meant beer not ammunition, and who, as far as anyone can tell,
never fired a shot, even by accident. It was a small spark thrown
off in the angry time of Tryweryn. In certain patriotic and well-
intentioned young men, incensed by Tryweryn and anxious to
do something positive for Wales, the Free Wales Army struck a
chord. That, in itself, might have been channelled elsewhere or
have spent itself in song and Mittyish dreaming in saloon bars
deep in Carmarthenshire, Cardiganshire and elsewhere.

But, unfortunately for the Free Wales Army and for the
serious nationalists who were from time to time stained by its
outrageous nonsense, its activities also struck a chord with
newspapers and magazines in Britain and Europe.

There were several reasons for this. The Free Wales Army
was noisily alive at the time that the determined and secret
saboteurs were blowing up pipelines and pushing alarm clocks

with dynamite into public buildings, in the name of Wales. Thus the question of Welsh extremism was not only serious, it was dramatic, too. It was properly a subject for discussion, investigation and report in newspapers and television programmes. Moreover, the great public relations exercise of the investiture of the Prince of Wales lay ahead: gelignited pipelines were interesting enough, in their way, but now the story had the magnetic royal angle to it and newspapers began to ask, 'Is Charles in danger?'

Garrulous members of the Free Wales Army were happy to half-admit responsibility for bomb outrages as part of a campaign to 'free Wales from the tyrannical English'. The painted slogans began to appear on bridges and walls up and down Wales and with them the representation of the Snowdon eagle, a device the Free Wales Army took as its emblem. The commandants of the army (there were no rank-and-file, only officers) would, when pressed, modestly put the strength of their army in the order of several hundreds or several thousands. It was a pity that some newspapers, whose influence was important, gave credence to the commandants, although most journalists in Wales knew the truth about the Free Wales Army and did not contribute to the fairy story. In the main it was the writers who came from England and the continent who did not bring with them that old-fashioned journalistic quality—scepticism. A combination of gullibility and the willingness to create a story of Celtic guerillas drilling and manoeuvring in the mountains, in readiness for the seizure of power, were enough to put the Free Wales Army on the map. Also, the paramilitary manifestations—Red Dragon flags, guerilla-style forage caps, green combat jackets embroidered FWA, Snowdon eagle badges—plus a ready flow of rhetoric, were hard for newspaper men sitting at desks many miles from Wales to ignore.

In the papers, and on the screen, the members of the Free Wales Army also fitted and perpetuated the image of the funny Welshman of music-hall fame. On a river of dramatic headlines and posed pictures, idle boasts and empty threats, the commandants rode headlong to their inevitable clash with the authorities. They were shown, in photographs, with rifles and pistols and what were said to be explosives. One published photograph purported to show FWA men and an explosion: the 'detonation' was a handful of dust thrown up in front of the camera by a co-operative commandant.

As the months went by and the investiture came nearer, the Free Wales Army became, increasingly, an embarrassment. The commandants openly expressed opposition to the investiture (like others in Wales) and they were publicly approving the bomb blasts at the same time as a Special Branch team was hard at work looking for those responsible; they were causing some anxiety by their constant encouragement of violent action. There was never any evidence to connect them with explosions, but they were teetering on the edge of dangerous ground.

The antics of the Free Wales Army were a continuing affront to the authorities. Some people felt that the talk of violence was adding a dangerous note to the anti-investiture feeling. Would the play-acting get out of hand? In security matters how much risk could be taken? In any case a well-organized demonstration on investiture day would be watched by half a billion people throughout the world. In the end it was a number of factors which led to the decision to risk making martyrs of the Free Wales Army leaders and bring them in. Approval for the arrests under the Public Order Act was given by the Attorney-General.

So it was that at six o'clock on the morning of 26 February 1969 there were knocks at the doors of nine homes throughout Wales. With some melodrama, which, in retrospect, appears to have been unnecessary, policemen arrested members of the Free Wales Army, searched their houses, drove them to the police station at Carmarthen, and charged them all with conspiracy. The authorities knew what they were, but treated them as if they were the determined guerilla chiefs of news-cutting fame and kept them in custody until trial.

One of them, Keith Griffiths, black-bearded and twenty-two years old, had been expecting the police to call. Hauled from sleep by the loud knocking he fumbled into trousers and muttered to his wife, Mair: 'This is the tea party they promised us.' A few weeks earlier a detective had told one of the commandants that there would be 'a tea party before the investiture'. And they took this to mean that by the time the Prince of Wales came to Caernarvon on July the first, a number of Free Wales Army men would be behind bars. Within a few minutes the police were in every room in the house, going through drawers, cupboards, personal effects, even the curtain linings. Griffiths was handcuffed. There were similar scenes in the eight other houses. In one a policeman atoned for waking children by giving them chocolate.

Into the police headquarters at Carmarthen went boxes of documents, posters, jackets, Castro caps, badges, a flag, a large painting. The nine men were charged with offences under the Public Order Act of 1936, a law prohibiting quasi-military organizations. But the police and the government knew perfectly well that the Free Wales Army was never an army. Welsh extremism has various shades—but the police had merely drawn the jokers from the pack and the knaves remained hidden.

The authorities now put on trial a group of Billy Liars, immature men with a weakness for exaggeration, patriots with a sincere love of Wales who channelled frustration into a game which was at first serious, became a joke, was exploited and misrepresented, and ended a thin and pathetic farce.

The Free Wales Army was first seen in public, in its rough and ready uniform, at the opening of the Tryweryn dam in October 1965. It consisted of a few men distributing leaflets and talking to reporters. Pamphlets had been passed around calling on 'the true sons of Wales to raise the flag and answer the call to arms'. There had been a spate of slogan painting, for the commandants' armoury was largely made up of brushes and white paint.

But in the newspapers and magazines of Britain, France and America, the Free Wales Army claimed a rapidly growing membership. Interviews were gladly given. There was always a welcome in the hillside for reporters and cameramen who scribbled down the rhetoric, photographed 'exercises' and filmed Karno-esque squarebashing. The group's leaders boasted of 2000 men ready to fight for Wales, even of heavy guns and aircraft hidden in the mountains.

But some of the spirit of the Free Wales Army was summed up in the facetious advertisement it inserted in a newspaper: 'Join the Free Wales Army. Subscription 5s. Old age pensioners 2s 6d.' *Eisteddfodau* were favourite meeting places and in the pubs around these very Welsh festivals a fair number joined the FWA, for as long as an hour or two, and more often than not with a pint in hand and two or three inside them. A few ardent patriots, believing what they had heard or read, came to join the colours. They must have been disappointed. Instead of an army there was a disorganized group, bolstering the talk with old guns, badges and Press cuttings. The meetings became sessions of clowning and patriotic songs. After one such meeting one of the leading commandants went home to his wife and wept at the disorganization of it all.

One of the commandants awarded himself the 'international Celtic cross of honour' and said he had won it for bravery on a bomb mission. Around all the activities of the FWA was a schoolboy Red Hand Gang atmosphere. There were the passwords and a fearsome oath which ended: 'I solemnly swear in the name of God and all our dead patriots that I shall never reveal any secrets of our organization even if I am captured and tortured. If I betray this faith I shall deserve the punishment of death as a traitor and may eternal contempt cover me.' There were songs, too, such as this one, based on an IRA song:

> Tramp, tramp, tramp the boys are marching
> To join up with the FWA.
> Underneath the Union Jack,
> Welshmen never can be free,
> So here's hoist *Ddraig Goch* [the Red Dragon]
> For Wales and liberty.

For *Plaid Cymru*, the Free Wales Army became an acute embarrassment: it was too easy for the party's enemies to associate the two, to talk of them in one breath. There was concern that serious nationalism was being damaged by the FWA and party officers were instructed to expel people connected with it.

With the investiture at Caernarvon looming large, one member of the Free Wales Army drew up exotic plans for war with England which was to break out on July the first, with

WALES AND THE WELSH

Caernarvon as the first target. The plans were but a daydream and suggested the use of model aeroplanes filled with explosives to attack the Royal Yacht *Britannia*, dogs with bombs on their backs trained to attack English tanks—kamikaze corgis?—and men swimming Caernarvon castle moat to put bombs under the walls. A blueprint for the 'battle of Caernarvon' began: 'If the Pretender is crowned our homeland dies. It is up to us to see that he is not. We call upon Welshmen to organize, train and equip, to arm themselves with guns, bombs, Molotov cocktails, grenades, pikes, bows and arrows, swords, bayonets, clubs . . . eggs filled with acid, flour and smoke bombs, nuts and bolts, sharpened pennies . . . Stock up and bring them to Caernarvon. The area within thirty miles of Caernarvon will be the battle zone. Engage the enemy on July the first, seize the castle at dawn. The flag of free Wales must fly from the castle that day. A Celtic legion has been established of volunteers ready to fight and die in Wales. . . . Squads will assassinate the Pretender if necessary and other key people on the black list.'

Six of the nine men were convicted and two of the leaders were sentenced to eighteen months in prison. They were hard sentences but there was, presumably, a need to exhibit the mailed fist. The judge said to the convicted men: 'However misguided you were I have taken into account that you were all lovers of Wales . . . I hope and believe I understand patriotism and the love of liberty. I hope, too, I understand the desire of men to improve the conditions of their fellows and their homeland. I know there is a Welsh way of life very dear to the people in this land of Wales. The right to hold dear the matters I have mentioned has not been on trial in this case. None of you has been charged with loving Wales. Just as there is a Welsh way of life, so there is a civilized and orderly way of life which is international and which is cherished by the people of other lands. And crime has no place in it. Some of you caused among your fellow countrymen anxiety and alarm by your schemes, claims and boastings and, in the case of two of you, weapons. You have served Wales ill. It is said on your behalf there is no evidence connecting you with any of the bomb incidents. What is not known is what encouragement your public boastings, public displays and private propaganda may have given to those who were. What is known is the approval some of you gave to evildoers and the encouragement for their future you offered.'

A few hours before the judge began the last speech of the trial, two men at Abergele, at the other end of Wales, had been blown to pieces by the bomb they were carrying. The judge called the three acquitted FWA men to him and said: 'There is too much violence. It is bad for Wales. You have been near danger and you have been playing with fire. Off you go and see if you can patch up the wounds that have been inflicted on the body of Wales.'

The trial of the Free Wales Army, which ended, by curious coincidence, on investiture day, ensured constant publicity and bestowed upon the group an importance it had never earned. There were many in Wales who said it was a show trial arranged for political motives, to damage the Welsh national movement, an allegation firmly denied by the judge. If the intention was to prove to the public that here was a gang of Welsh desperadoes, the move failed. It was a strange business altogether, but, at best, it helped to clear the air in Wales. The trial lasted for ten weeks, provided employment for eight Queen's Counsel and nine junior counsel, and cost more than £100,000 of public money. It was an elaborate and expensive way of dealing with toy soldiers.

# 8 The gelignitist

The Free Wales Army played it partly for make-believe, and
the fun of it, and let it get out of hand. John Barnard Jenkins
played it wholly for real. Like others he saw Wales as a small
and oppressed country—his own country—whose values were
being crushed. And he reacted. 'The military, political and
economic wars have long been lost in Wales and the final
cultural annihilation has been slowly, insidiously and fatally
gathering momentum,' he wrote later. But the form that his
reaction took made him a rare exception. As the self-styled
director-general of a group he called *Mudiad Amddiffyn Cymru*, or
Movement for the Defence of Wales, he was responsible for
many of the explosions which damaged water pipelines and
government buildings in Wales and along the border between
1966 and 1969. In 1970, at the assize court at Mold in Flintshire
he was charged with nineteen offences involving explosions and
explosives. At first he denied them all, but eventually pleaded
guilty to eight. The prosecution agreed not to proceed on six
others and the jury formally brought in verdicts of not guilty on
the rest. John Jenkins was sent to prison for ten years. The wild
periods of bombs and tension which led, inevitably, to the
horrifying deaths of two men, and the maiming of a little boy,
was at an end.

In a letter from prison to some friends, Jenkins said that he
'took up arms' because, with many other people, he felt
instinctively that the Welsh national identity—'our sacred soul,
our everything'—was not only being threatened but was in the
last stages of survival.

'Our old Mother Wales . . . is not a beautiful young girl after
whom I lust, or an old duchess whose money and status I
desire; she is old, well past her best, decrepit, boozy, and has
taken strange bedfellows without the saving grace of desperation . . . I owe her my love and my loyalty, she is my mother.
She may be a liability but is the sort of liability that a crippled
child is, in the eyes of its parents. If I ignore her in her hour of

need no one will ever know or condemn, except myself, and I have the sort of conscience that stops functioning the moment I stop breathing.'

Jenkins's counsel at his trial said: 'This man was not motivated by greed or self-interest. He was motivated by a deep, intense concern for Wales and for the future of Wales.' This is certainly true. Although he had delusions of grandeur, Jenkins did—does—care passionately for Wales and found ample evidence to back his firmly-held belief that his country was being sapped and destroyed. Although not a speaker of the Welsh language he was intensely concerned for it. In a letter from prison he said: 'Force is to diplomacy what bullion is to banknotes. I have always believed that there is a direct connection between one's social attitude towards a people, and its fighting record.' 'The fight is not only against inertia and apathy but against time itself, because *Cymraeg* [Welsh] can only be saved and a cultural renaissance created by an Independent Welsh Government, and, if by the time such a Government exists, the proportion of Welsh-speakers has reached a certain level, then, as the Irish have found out, there is nothing that can be done to save it, or it can only hope for an expensive and artificial prolongation. . . .'

He also explained in another letter from Wormwood Scrubs, what made him take to bombs: 'There are still those who believe that I was waging a physical war to achieve some sort of military victory, that in fact I intended among other things to deny water to the large English conurbations. As people who understand these things now know, the strategy was military, to achieve a short term mental attitude leading to a long term political settlement. The fight was not to stop water but to create a state of mind. . . .'

The director-general of *Mudiad Amddiffyn Cymru* must, at times, have felt himself secure beyond capture. For three years he had things very much his own way. Police and Special Branch officers intensified their search for the perpetrator of the bomb blasts but Jenkins, able to strike as and when he chose, was a fleeting shadow. He remained unsuspected for a long time because he was an efficient sergeant in the British Army and used the Army as a cover throughout his operations.

John Jenkins was born at Penbryn, Glamorgan, in 1933, and spent part of his life in the mining village of Aberfan, near Merthyr Tydfil. The disaster of Aberfan in 1966 had a traumatic effect on him. It is reasonable to assume that the disaster hardened his resolve even more. When he was told about the horror of that time by his brother-in-law, who was a rescuer at Aberfan, Jenkins became 'insensate with grief' and began to drink heavily and complain bitterly about the authorities.

Mr Tasker Watkins, VC, QC, who prosecuted at his trial, said that the sergeant was a clever and ruthless fanatic who had been concerned in twelve explosions and two attempts to cause explosions. 'He believed independence in Wales can only be achieved by violence and he scorns any peaceful and constitutional means of achieving that end. The whole story of his life during the past five years has been one of complete addiction to this form of dangerous violence.'

Jenkins, who joined the Royal Army Dental Corps in 1950 as a dental clerk, earned praise from his superiors for the neat and military-efficient way he kept the stores at the Army Dental Centre at Saighton Camp, Chester. It was in the stores that he made some of the parts for his bombs and bored the holes for the parts with Army dental drills. For eighteen months he also kept about 150 pounds of gelignite, stored in an ordnance depot packing case. On one occasion some Army bomb disposal experts borrowed some of the equipment from the stores, including mirrors on rods, to investigate Jenkins's own explosive contraptions.

The sergeant's Army work was not confined to the dental stores. He was also allowed to serve as an instructor to the Corps of Drums of a Territorial battalion of the Royal Welsh Fusiliers in Wrexham where he lived in married quarters. Sometimes he stored explosives in his garage.

During 1967 a young man called Frederick Alders joined the TA as a trainee flautist, and consequently met Sergeant Jenkins. Alders, too, was a man concerned at what was happening to Wales and the Aberfan disaster had affected him strongly and convinced him that 'something' should be done. Before long Alders was admitted to *Mudiad Amddiffyn Cymru* and Sergeant Jenkins administered an oath of allegiance, an event which even Alders thought rather strange because it occurred in the all-ranks' mess of an Army barracks with an Army sergeant, Jenkins, officiating at the proceedings.

About the end of 1968 Jenkins heard that the police were making a check on the sales of Venner time switches. The sergeant had been using these for his explosive devices: they were fairly easily purchased and very reliable. But as soon as he heard about the police inquiries he stopped using the Venner switches and began making his own. He used alarm clocks; he removed the minute hand and arranged for the circuit between the battery and the detonator to be completed when the hour hand of the clock touched a wire inserted through a small aperture in the glass. Providing that the devices were set up in situ, and with care, they were safe enough. There was danger, however, if the bomb switches were set in motion before being taken to their target. If the clock was knocked or allowed to slip on its face there was a chance that the bomb would explode prematurely.

Some of Sergeant Jenkins's gelignite, which had been stolen from a colliery store near Wrexham, began to 'sweat'. Nitro-glycerine started to weep out of it and, as people who are familiar with explosives know, this is a warning that the stick of gelignite should be disposed of. . . .

During the small hours of July the first, the day of the investiture, two Welshmen, anxious to make a demonstration for Wales, set off from their homes at Abergele, Denbighshire, carrying a Jenkins bomb. William Alwyn Jones and George Francis Taylor, who both had young children, presumably intended to put the bomb in the civic offices at Abergele which were close by the railway line on which would travel the train carrying many members of the Royal family to Caernarvon.

Maybe the holdall bag in which the bomb lay bumped against a wall or a knee; perhaps the device had been pre-set and the clock tipped over; the sweating nitro-glycerine might have needed very little to detonate it; no one knows exactly what happened. But in an instant the two men were dead, and the explosion rocked the street. At the trial the jury was advised not to look at the photographs of the result.

Two years later Jenkins wrote from prison: 'It is a highly

significant fact that the two National Welsh Martyrs who died at Abergele were not Welsh-speaking, but I affirm that they truly loved the Welsh language.' He wrote this in an examination of the position of 'the *Cymro di-Gymraeg* (the Welshman who does not speak Welsh) without whom no answers to the problems of Wales are possible . . . those who, like myself, are Welsh but not Welsh-speaking and English-speaking but not English . . . these are the people who are going to determine the Welsh future because of their numerical preponderance. [There is] an extra dimension of deprivation suffered by the latter (and there are many of them) which tends to drive them to an insane fury when the language is slighted in any way.'

A few days after the Abergele explosion, a boy of ten, on holiday with his parents, kicked a ball over the wall at the back of an ironmonger's shop in Caernarvon. He went to retrieve it, set off a bomb and suffered a severe leg injury. It was apparent that the bomb had been meant as an investiture day explosion, for the shop was on the processional route . . . and a large crowd of people had been close to it.

The death of two men and the injury to a child was the turn of the tide for Sergeant Jenkins. There was a difference between a hole in a pipeline carrying Welsh water to England and blood on the pavement. A few people began to talk. The police, already making an intensive search for the shadowy men behind the bomb blasts, redoubled their effort. A team of fifteen detectives from the Gwynedd (North Wales) and the Cheshire police forces was set up to track the director-general of the Movement for the Defence of Wales. Dozens of people were interviewed or watched and the pieces of information in the files re-scrutinized.

In the files was an account of a curious meeting between three journalists, Ian Skidmore, Harold Pendlebury and Emyr Jones, and three members of *Mudiad Amddiffyn Cymru*. The meeting, in 1968, took place in a darkened room. Two of the three MAC men were Sergeant Jenkins and Alders. The reporters were told that the group had started in 1963 but had taken its present form in 1967. Jenkins said: '*Plaid Cymru* is too saintly to recognize the facts of life. We want to draw attention to the plight of Wales and win the support of the people. . . .

We are prepared to kill. The aim is to make the government sit up and take notice.'

As the police inquiry intensified, a girl remembered that two Territorial Army men who had been at a St David's Day ceremony near Ruthin were the men she had seen making a bomb in a backyard. . . . A man who had been given two Jenkins bombs decided that matters had gone far enough with the Abergele deaths, and he helped the police.

Three months after the investiture the police decided to visit Sergeant Jenkins because his name had appeared a number of times in the pile of information at the investigation centre. After a pleasant enough interview, Jenkins panicked and took a case of explosives from the dental store at his barracks and moved them to Alders's home in Wrexham—the home into which newly-married Alders had just moved with his bride. One week later, at dawn on a Sunday morning, police arrived at the house and began to search it. In a cupboard beside the fireplace in the living room they found alarm clocks, batteries, detonators and wire, and a cache of gelignite. The explosive had deteriorated and, after one glance, a bomb disposal team took it away and destroyed it.

Alders had become convinced that Jenkins had been mad to go on planning more bombings after the Abergele tragedy and he arranged for the next bomb he was given to fail. Just before the trial he turned Queen's evidence and, for his part in the short and tense era when desperate Welshmen turned to violence, he was imprisoned for six years.

Passing sentence on the two, Mr Justice Thompson, told them: 'The motives prompting you were not personal gain but a misguided motive that you were patriotically promoting the interests of Wales. You were not. Wales will disclaim and disown such methods of promoting her interests. She will condemn the terror you contrived to spread by your wicked deeds.'

In a letter from his cell, Jenkins said: 'Of course it can be said that violence is unnecessary and that *Plaid Cymru* have the answer. To this I would agree; there is no doubt that Wales will inevitably become independent. My proviso is that by the time independence arrives the Wales we know and hate/love even now will have long gone; the Wales we wanted Free and Welsh will be absolutely unattainable. . . . At least, all that I was prepared to sacrifice was my life and my freedom for my ideals. I oppose the leaders of *Plaid Cymru* because they are prepared to sacrifice their people, their country and their heritage, on the shrine of their respectability and pacifism.'

# 9 Pieces of the weave

The view from my window is of the soft and wooded interlocking hills, the cottages and buttercup meadows of the Vale of Glamorgan. In the background the landscape fades into blue hills and behind them, around to the north-west, is the mighty Rhondda. In the centreground, bold against the sky, resting on a high saddle between two bosom hills, is the little town of Llantrisant, identified by the tower of its church and the crumbled butt of its ruined castle. It is a natural fortress, with a commanding view over the Vale of Glamorgan which unfolds dramatically towards the south and ends at the beaches of what in English is known as the Bristol Channel, and what in Welsh is called the Severn Sea.

The hillside on which Llantrisant is built is a second-gear job. Puffing walkers have the sympathy of the ghosts of those soldiers who fought around Llantrisant over the centuries, who found this same hill such a breathless haul and left the ground damp with their sweat and sword-tapped blood. Llantrisant, which means the church of three saints, is a bit dog-eared these days, like a frontier town that has known slightly better times, and it needs a lick of paint. It is picturesque, though, and leans on its history and, for a little place, has quite enough fame to be getting on with.

I can see, close by the town, the field known as Caerlan, where Dr William Price, the remarkable Victorian hippy and raiser of decent chapel folk's eyebrows, set fire to the body of his infant son, Jesus Christ. His acquittal, and the judge's remarks, at his subsequent trial established the legality of cremation in Britain. If the events set down in this short synopsis were to happen today, news editors' hands would flick as fast as vipers' tongues to the 'phones and the editorial commandos would be dispatched to Llantrisant from London and the corners of the planet.

Dr Price was well known in Wales for his eccentric ways and his fondness for litigation which became almost a hobby. A brilliant man, by all accounts, but a schizophrenic, he would stalk about the countryside, his white beard and mane flowing, dressed in a distinctive green costume he designed himself, with a scarlet scalloped waistcoat. Sometimes he wore a plaid shawl and a fox skin cap, with the forelegs dangling over his brow, so that he appeared like a Celtic Davy Crockett.

He was born at Ty'nycoedcae, Rudry, in Glamorgan, in 1800, of a schizophrenic father and an illiterate mother. He qualified as a doctor at the age of twenty and started to practise in South Wales. As a natural radical he became a determined member of the Chartist movement during the time of industrial unrest in the 1830s and planned armed rebellion. But in the Chartist troubles of 1839 he had to flee Wales, disguised as a woman, and stayed in Paris until the heat was off.

Dr Price loved Wales deeply. He defended the country, its language and traditions and spoke out against the spoiling of the countryside. He became fanatically interested in druidism and Welsh culture—and the *Modern English Biography* of 1897 noted that he 'studied ancient Welsh literature so assiduously that his mind became weakened'. He was a sun worshipper and officiated at druidic ceremonies at the rocking stones above Pontypridd. Here, he baptized his first child, whom he called the Countess of Glamorgan.

He spurned convention, to the outrage of the strongly chapel-minded. He said that 'matrimony is to be mercilessly condemned as an institution which reduces the fair sex to a condition of slavery'. However, he went through a 'druidic marriage' with his young housekeeper Gwenllian Llewellyn, when he was eighty-one, and had three children by her. The family lived in a small cottage in Llantrisant.

He had a reputation as a healer: people tended to go to him when all else had failed. The stories of his medical prowess are legion; some are true, no doubt, and the rest make a fair stack of apocrypha. To some patients he said firmly: 'Do as I say and you will get well; if you don't you will die.' He loathed smoking and refused to take on a patient unless he promised to give up the habit. Once, on a train from Pontypridd to Merthyr Tydfil, he asked a fellow passenger to stop smoking and, when the man refused, tore the pipe away and threw it out of the window. He was a vegetarian, did not believe in vaccination, was a phenomenal walker, never wore socks because he believed they were unhealthy, and was so fastidiously clean that he washed coins before putting them in his pockets.

Dr Price's eccentricities, his litigation and his druidic rites made him alarming or unspeakable in the eyes of many people. But on the Sunday evening of 13 January 1884, he committed the ultimate outrage that had the local community bubbling with anger.

People were coming away from chapel when they noticed a fire atop the hill at Caerlan Field. There was the doctor, in his long white robe, a Welsh chant upon his lips, burning the body of his five-months-old son Iesu Grist (the Welsh form of Jesus Christ) in a barrel of oil. As the knot of curious people thickened, Sergeant William Hoyle of the local police arrived and kicked the cask over. The blazing body of the baby rolled out. The crowd, now certain they were witnessing human sacrifice, were furious. In the face of their hostility the doctor was lodged in the local cells.

At the inquest in Llantrisant Dr Price was permitted to take away his son's body on condition that he buried it. On the way home he stopped off at a shed to feed his cow. A number of people had followed him and now, ears to the door, they listened. Inside, Dr Price was chopping up swedes for the cow, but to the listeners it sounded as if he was chopping up the baby. When the doctor came out he was stoned and had to flee to the Bear Inn for safety. Meanwhile a mob gathered outside his cottage and began to pelt it. Gwenllian, a pistol in each hand, faced the crowd and said she would shoot the first man who tried to enter. She looked as if she meant it and the people drifted away.

From the magistrates' court at Pontypridd the doctor was sent for trial at Glamorgan Assizes and there, on 12 February 1884, he was accused of attempting to burn the body of his child, instead of burying it, and attempting to burn the body with intent to prevent the holding of an inquest. He pleaded not guilty and defended himself. He was acquitted after Mr Justice Stephen said that a person who burned a body instead of burying it did not commit a criminal act. Dr Price celebrated, naturally, by suing the police for defamation and wrongful arrest and won a farthing in damages.

Meanwhile, he had kept his son's body under his bed. He cremated it at Caerlan, on a coal pyre, in March 1884.

The incredible doctor remained spry and vigorous almost to the last—he fathered a daughter at the age of eighty-six—but in his final months grew weaker and took to drinking champagne to perk himself up. At last, in January 1893, he lay dying in his cottage. He asked for a glass of champagne, drank it and died.

He had often said: 'Don't place me in the ground.' He had been fascinated by fire and believed in cremation not merely for reasons of hygiene. He had marked the place of his own cremation at Caerlan with a pole sixty-one feet high and gave detailed instructions in his will for his disposal 'when I shall cease to be in my present tenement called . . . William Price'.

His cremation was no quiet affair. Llantrisant was packed. There was a rush for tickets and among the applicants were many doctors and ministers of religion. The tickets were inscribed: 'Tuesday, Jan 31 '93: Cremation of Dr Price. Admit bearer. Gwenllian Llewellyn.' The large crowd, between 6000 and 20,000 strong according to different reports, was quiet and there were thirty-five policemen on duty. A pyre of stone and brick had been constructed at Caerlan, fuelled by coal and timber. It was designed to burn the body without exposing the coffin to the watchers. The coffin itself was of iron, with holes for the flames to enter, and twelve bearers carried it to the pyre. When the fire cooled, souvenir hunters picked up pieces of the coffin which had shattered, and later there were pictures and illustrated scarves for sale depicting the doctor and the final act which was as spectacular as his personality and his life. The town hasn't been quite the same since!

Llantrisant had a charter in 1346 and still has a court leet and a body of freemen who meet for a dinner every year, when they put on their green and black ties and drink port from a silver loving cup. Llantrisant men are still called 'the Black Army'— the nickname their ancestors earned for their service under the Black Prince in the wars in France.

The name of the little town has become much more widely

known recently as the home of the new Royal Mint. People who did not want to see the London Mint transferred from Tower Hill to Wales, largely out of an anti-provincial feeling, unkindly referred to Llantrisant as the hole with the Mint. The joke is now spent. The Mint building itself is remarkable only for its outstanding dullness.

Maybe, as Llantrisant leans upon its history, it is merely drawing breath. There is a scheme afoot to make it the dignified focus of a new town. The theory is that this would be a vital growth centre, able to attract the kind of industrial development South Wales badly needs. But there are those with great doubts, who feel that dreaming glass and concrete spires and housing estates and factory settlements at Llantrisant could only suck the economic blood from the nearby valleys. The debate proceeds.

I go by way of Llantrisant on my way to the middle and the north of Wales. The road goes to Pontypridd, then past Aberfan and its twin community of Merthyr Vale. Aberfan today is rejoining the world. I suppose that one of the most remarkable things about this little place is that the people did not flee from it in their grief. Other communities elsewhere would have been crushed beyond repair, but these valley communities have a great capacity for fighting.

For all the social and psychiatric help in the years after the disaster, the main underpinning of the community's life was done by the people themselves. Indeed, the story of this town's self-help is one of the inspiring stories of Aberfan, to be set alongside all the dreadful and unspeakable events surrounding the disaster and the unhappy early months of the enormous (and embarrassing because of its enormity) disaster fund. Five years after the collapse of tip number seven, the six tips that remained on the mountainside were at last removed. It was a pity that some politicians and others made themselves appear so hard by refusing, at first, to have the remaining black scabs removed at once from the mountainside. The people had to fight to get it done.

The place where the tips stood is now covered with grass. But you cannot expect the scarring to fade from people's minds. Many of the children who survived are getting over the shock:

they have the resilience of youth on their side. But the disaster will always be a pain for the adults.

'The scar is always there,' a man said, as we contemplated the memorial garden on the land where the school once stood, 'and a word, a noise, a snatch of song, a shout, is enough to bring it all back. The misery, the injustice of it all. Sudden death was always a part of going into the pit—God knows we have learned that in these valleys—but not of going to school.'

Now the road goes through bustling Merthyr with its big hard memories and its present fears and, at last, into the Brecon Beacons where the sheep have the not-amused expressions of dry old ladies as they rise reluctantly from the cats'-eyes, and the hawks hang in the air monitoring the moorland for an entrée. In pleasant Brecon there is an old cigarette machine built into a wall and the price of the Players is not written on card, to be changed almost month by month, it is engraved in solid metal letters and calls back a time before my time: sixpence a packet.

The road to the salmon-catchers' town of Builth Wells runs beside the River Wye; you should see the might of the river in the early spring after great rain, when it comes charging down all brown and full and looking for trouble. In quieter times it pushes around the rocks and a tall heron is on sentry-go on a midstream boulder and keeps a look-out for his lunch. After Builth the countryside gets wider and wilder and the river becomes thinner, a silvery winding thread, as the road climbs up to Plynlimon.

Away from the armour of the car, up here on Plynlimon, the sensation of timelessness and remoteness is intense. In winter, with the thin afternoon sunlight being bullied away, there is a kind of loneliness and a natural hostility that I can recommend if you feel like being put in your place.

After Plynlimon there is Aberystwyth, one of my favourite Welsh towns. It has the rounded and self-contained qualities of a large village and, indeed, one of its 10,000 people, who would not move if you promised him the chair and crown at the national *eisteddfod*, described it to me as the nearest equivalent in Britain to the independent city states of ancient Greece.

It lies in the bow of Cardigan Bay, a long way from the

influences of the large towns; Shrewsbury and Swansea are more than sixty miles off and Cardiff is a three hour drive. So Aberystwyth keeps its distance and its Welsh character; and this character in spite of the tide of holidaymakers. The Welsh language exists easily alongside abrasive Wolverhampton and Birmingham accents, and in the shops you are still more likely to get a *diolch yn fawr* with your change than a thank-you.

Somehow Aberystwyth has managed to keep faith with its past. The sweep of the promenade, the distinctive crescent of nineteenth-century houses and hotels, the knobbly trees growing in the streets, give Aber an old-fashioned charm. Its air is of a watering place from which the bathing machines and dimpled belles have but lately vanished and the visiting cards of gentlemen still lie on hall tables. Aber made an early move to respectability. A writer once praised it for placing the men's and women's bathing machines 'nearly a quarter mile asunder', thus avoiding 'the indecency of promiscuous dipping so disgusting at more fashionable resorts'.

The town's chapels still have a fair measure of status. Chapel-going has declined, of course, as it has everywhere in Wales, but some chapels in the town still have a good attendance and those who are judges of such matters assure me that some of the best preaching in the country can be heard from the town's pulpits.

You won't find a night club in Aberystwyth, no Cymric croupiers and chemmy shoes; nothing so big city. That kind of decadence does not fit the town's style of life. But if you hanker after a little of the devil's works there are some slot machines, concessions to our sinful times, and rather shamefaced they look, too. Do not get the wrong impression: Aber is not a strait-laced and frowning place. It likes its fun, all right, but it likes the even tenor of its life. There are some lively bars and lively times to be had in them. The liveliness stems largely from the 3000-strong student population. They are at the University of Wales college and they make up a quarter of the overall population and give Aberystwyth the kind of vigorous atmosphere that lifts it out of the run of small seaside towns. In 1971 Aber became the first town in Britain to admit students to the policy-making committees of its council. A few people let their generation gap show and frowned on the notion, but, bathed in enlightenment, the council co-opted three students and gave them full voting rights.

One of the prides of Aberystwyth is the pride of Wales, the *Llyfrgell Genedlaethol Cymru*, the national library, built between 1911 and 1955, and the home of the greatest collection of Welsh manuscripts and books.

Here, among the sacred tomes, a small team of lexicographers is patiently ploughing the furrow from A to U (no K, J, Q, V, X or Z in the Welsh alphabet) in the compilation of the definitive Welsh dictionary—a counterpart of the Oxford English Dictionary. This work was, in fact, inspired by the Oxford, which took seventy years to compile, and the job was launched by the Board of Celtic Studies in 1921. There is a cautious hope among these patient fellows at the national library that the great dictionary, which will have more than 100,000 words, will be finished in 1985, or thereabouts, and when I last spoke to them they were working their way through H.

Ten miles from Aberystwyth, in the valley known as Cwmrheidol, I walked into the heart of a mountain, 1500 feet through a dripping tunnel, to see some prospectors drilling into a lead vein. Many parts of Wales have good deposits of lead, zinc, copper and other minerals, including a little silver and gold, and in the past two years there has been a great increase in prospecting activity. The world's enormous appetite for minerals has forced mining companies to go to those places, like Wales, where modern techniques make it worthwhile to go for lower grade ores. Wales has a long tradition of metal mining: the Romans used slaves to hack out the lead and gold of Cardiganshire and Merioneth eighteen centuries ago. Welsh gold has an almost mystic quality. It is the stuff of dreams and royal wedding rings. In the Merioneth gold rush of the nineteenth century, twenty-four mines were dug and gold worth about £1 million was brought out.

It now seems likely that Wales will become a useful metal-producing area and there is a hope in some rural districts that mining jobs will slow the drift away from the countryside. On the other hand there is concern that giant open-cast operations will do irreparable harm to matchless landscape. It is a very large argument, involving the familiar conservationists *v.*

industrialists battle, unemployment and the erosion of Welsh communities.

To travel from Aberystwyth to the north, with time to spare, is a marvellous indulgence, for the landscape is a song all the way. The road, the direct road, goes through Machynlleth, chosen by Owain Glyndwr as the capital of Wales, where, at the height of the Welsh rebellion, he was proclaimed the King of Wales, and where his parliament house still stands; across the Dovey valley, so beautiful it leaves the garrulous speechless and makes the taciturn babble; through the slate district of Corris, all black and glistening like an anthracite alligator; through Dolgellau, dignified, solid, enduring. The centuries roll away and the warriors' mountains and the serpentine trails of the ancient Celts are yours.

If you take the Trawsfynydd road, or the coast road through Harlech, you will reach the little corner, in the angle made by the Lleyn peninsula and the Merioneth coast, which is called Tremadoc Bay. Lloyd George lived here, in Criccieth, and is buried nearby at Llanystumdwy; Bertrand Russell lived here, in Minffordd, in a house on a bluff between the gaunt mountains he walked over as a young man, and the sea. This was for many years his anchorage and, ultimately, it was his deathplace. It was his pleasure to sit or lie on his bed to watch the sun setting over Tremadoc Bay and, the evening he died, his last sight was of the darkening sea and sky.

Here, too, in this corner, is Portmeirion, a magic place. People often ask: 'What is Portmeirion?' and the simple answer is that it is a village. But the real answer is that it is a personal experience, an atmosphere, a fragile spell. It is an invented, enchanted gingerbread village and to enjoy it fully you must bring your imagination and sense of fun on the trip. It is the kind of place where you expect something romantic or curious or splendid to happen.

I awoke one May morning at Portmeirion and drew back the curtains to see the estuary, the caramel sand, the Rhinog mountains, the woods and the sea—alive and as sharp as steel in the early sunshine. It was breathtaking. And Portmeirion itself, still and still-slumbering, winding like a vine up the cliffside, seemed to have its own light and magic air. I expected, at the very least, to see Excalibur wet and glinting over the water, or pirates with muffled oars and moidores, or even the Queen of Hearts. Instead, on a nearby balcony, there was a life-size figure of William Shakespeare giving me an amused and endless look.

The man who made Portmeirion, its artist, impresario and master of ceremonies, is Sir Clough Williams-Ellis. Tall, commanding, unmistakable, strong, he favours knee breeches and yellow stockings, a bow tie, a broad brimmed hat, a blackened chipped pipe that looks as if it has suffered a whiff of grapeshot. He is a descendant of Gruffudd ap Cynan, a twelfth-century king of northern Wales; he is a noted designer of buildings, a town and country planner, dedicated conservationist who was thumping tubs for the environment long before pollution became a dirty word, and the oldest practising architect in Britain. When I first saw him he said: 'I shall be a hundred years old in twelve years' time.' He and his wife, the writer Amabel Williams-Ellis, do not live in Portmeirion; they are at the seventeenth-century ancestral home, Plas Brondanw, a few miles away, where they gave me a memorable day: lunch and a briefing on Portmeirion, a conducted tour, a stream of anecdotes and quotations, tea beside the log fire, then a typewriter and some paper.

Portmeirion formed in Clough Williams-Ellis's boyhood imaginings and, later, he cast around for a peaceful corner where he could make the dream a reality. He searched for a while and then 'discovered' the land at Portmeirion, more or less on his doorstep, and already a garden. In 1925, on the hillside which slopes to the beach, he began to indulge his yearning to create a village. Over the years, under his light-opera direction, it grew and is now almost finished. Towers, courts, colonnades, fountains, belvederes, arches, walls, houses, steps and paths, a dome and shops, sculptures, urns and cobbles, rescued façades and ceilings, are all disposed with rhythm and symmetry among the azaleas, hydrangeas, rhododendrons, palms, cypresses and eucalyptus of a marvellous wild garden. From every seat, window, door, balcony and corner there is a happy aspect. The fabled little town lies somewhere between Camelot and Xanadu, with a tincture of Portofino and Clovelly.

The village earns its living through its waterfront hotel, restaurants, from the little houses and cottages where visitors stay, and the admission fees paid by day visitors. The entrance fee varies and is raised and lowered to control the tide of visitors, like a sluice gate. Sir Clough confesses: 'The economic success of Portmeirion has staggered me. People tut-tutted at the beginning. Called it a mad escapade.'

Portmeirion's enchanted air has always drawn writers and artists: Steinbeck, Bertrand Russell, Daphne du Maurier, Compton Mackenzie, H. G. Wells and Shaw have stayed and worked here, and Noël Coward wrote *Blithe Spirit* in one week at Portmeirion.

On one of the cobbled walks of his kingdom, Sir Clough paused. 'It was Bernard Shaw who summed up some of my philosophy, in the words of the dying artist in *The Doctor's Dilemma*: "I believe in Michelangelo, Velasquez and Rembrandt; in the might of design, the mystery of colour, the redemption of all things by beauty everlasting. . . ." Portmeirion is an unashamedly romantic place and expresses what I feel. It is anti-brutalist and shows that it is possible to develop even a very beautiful landscape without defiling it. You see, I felt it was sad that so many people were missing so much through not appreciating town planning, colour and landscape. I wanted them to be able to find architecture entertaining and fun. Now people may criticize and say that I'm an old romantic, anti-modernist and backward looking. But even the moderns of the most severe rectitude come to Portmeirion for a good old wallow.

'I have a great admiration for the modern architects who have to tackle complex problems, and I only wish I could like what they build. Their work seems to me to be so unfeeling.'

Sir Clough Williams-Ellis has strong views about this. 'I have tried to persuade my brethren that men are not machines but soft and tender little animals. These modern buildings—they have firmness and commodity all right. But no feeling for humanity. It is sad. Delight has evaporated. So many places have been ruined by mishandling of their natural assets. What makes me angry is that planners and designers are neglecting great opportunities to create warmth and human interest. At

K

Portmeirion I have shown that architectural good manners can be good business. I fight for beauty.

'I have a dread vision of mechanized men in a macadamized desert. Our planners are fighting a losing battle, but what can they do against the odds? When I see what is happening in our towns and countryside I look into the future and think I am glad I shall not be there.'

The village now has the protection of the law because of its historical and architectural interest. Even its creator cannot touch it without permission from the Ministry. That appeals to his sense of humour. His puckish sense of fun and delight with life are found throughout the village. There is, for example, a plaque bearing a salutation to days of golden sunshine. It reads: 'To the summer of 1959 in honour of its splendour.' And now, another one: 'To the summer of 1971. Highly commended.'

Twenty miles or so to the north, beside the Menai Strait, is Caernarvon, possessor of the most magnificent castle in Britain. This was built between 1285 and 1322, a mighty and daunting fortress to show the Welsh that the English were the bosses and intended to keep it that way. When I go to Caernarvon today the sight of the castle calls back the last days of June and the first day of July in 1969, the atmosphere of carnival, the fine madness and the sniff of tension in the air.

The investiture of the Prince of Wales did not have the unanimous support of the people of Wales: some saw it as a colourful Celtic colony, a theatrical turn. There were lapel badges inscribed 'No Englishman is Prince of Wales'. The slogan 'Llewelyn Lives!' was scratched up on walls. (The last native Prince of Wales, Llewelyn II, was killed in battle three years before the foundations of Caernarvon's great castle were laid.) What with demonstrations, bomb blasts and other rumblings, the state carnival had to be surrounded by one of the greatest peacetime security operations.

The newly painted, spick and spanned and teeming town was packed to its gunwales and from the crowded pubs, into the milling street scenes, emerged those who sought respite from shoulder to shoulder drinking. The walls of the pubs and hotels took some time to lose their pregnant bulges.

Security was absolute. I was walking with a friend close by

the castle the day before the big day. He had a briefcase. Two serious men in dark suits materialized like Aladdin's genie, blotted out the sunshine and asked to see inside the briefcase, to make sure the contents were cheese-and-tomato, not gelignite. Even the violinists of the BBC Welsh Orchestra had to open up their violin cases for a frisking. On the big day the tension was there like a low cloud. The detectives were the men in smart suits who weren't smiling; they were up on the roofs with binoculars, spying out from narrow embrasures, watching hard. Out on the water beside the castle a group of bobbies bobbed in a rubber boat, their helmets jammed on firmly. There was some lightweight trouble: an egg splattered against the Queen's coach and some young men who had shouted and made V-signs were hauled off, with women in the crowd hissing at them. A small bomb or two went off in the distance, as a sort of gesture. It wasn't the happiest of days but, inside the castle, the ceremonial kernel of what was, for a day, the greatest show on earth, witnessed by half a billion people around the planet, transcended the ballyhoo and politicking, and achieved a simple dignity. That was one of the most remarkable things about it all.

From the north-west now, down the coast to the south-west and the charm of Pembrokeshire. The landscape here is more easy-going than the north's: the Preseli mountains do not have the sheer majesty and craggy might of the peerless giants of Snowdonia. They have a more homely beauty and their wildness looks more tamable. For grandeur on a larger scale in this region you must gaze at the coastscape; sensational by any standard.

Pembrokeshire's coast is a gruyère, pitted with holes and havens, coves and crannies, custom-made for running a little brandy and baccy ashore. One of the pleasant nooks is Lower Fishguard, where the River Gwaun enters the sea.

It is a picture of softly-dipping boats, a stone bridge and little quayside cottages, with Welsh dressers and gleaming plates. The piecrust roofs are manned by seagulls. There is the remnant of what was once a good fishing trade and you can still hear the old cry as the boats come in: '*Scadan Abergwaun*—Fishguard herrings.' Best not, for the time being, mention the name of Lower Fishguard in the town of Laugharne, in the next-door county of Carmarthen. Lower Fishguard was chosen by film-makers as their Llaregyb when they were looking for a location for *Under Milk Wood*. With the aid of a little art and pinkwash the film company transformed the place into the village which Dylan Thomas filled with the stuff of his dreams.

In Laugharne, where the poet worked and is buried, this caused a little hurt. The people there have always thought of their town as the model for Llaregyb. Still, as a man in Lower Fishguard said to me, with devastating logic, after I had told him of Laugharne's indignation: 'Well, I can't say that I have actually read *Under Milk Wood*, but our village must be the right place or Richard Burton wouldn't be here.'

Richard Burton, from the village of Pontrhydyfen, near Port Talbot, looking a little heavier and richer than in the days when he used to turn out for his local rugby side, was indeed there. But the local people, although duly impressed by the presence of the man, let it be known that they were not entirely inexperienced in the ways of film-makers. '*Moby Dick* was made here, you know, and we had Gregory Peck up and down all the time and that white whale out in the bay.' The film people were captivated. One of them lunched off *cawl*, the traditional Welsh broth, and his eyes grew dreamy. 'This food, it's soul food, and this place, it's so real, and the people here, they're real, too.'

Lower Fishguard lies at the bottom of the hill on which stands the main town of Fishguard. This is the port for Rosslare and Cork and the steamer link with Eire gives the town a pleasant blend of Welsh and Irish. Many Irishmen have settled here and Irish money circulates freely. 'This town is the famous terminal of the Guinness pipeline,' a Welshman said, buying me a pint of the stuff with Irish coin.

The ferry terminal is about a mile from the town and marks one of Fishguard's great disappointments. The quays and break-waters were built for Atlantic liners and there was every prospect of a golden age, but the war put an end to the scheme. Apart from the visits of film-makers there has not been much in the way of excitement here since the eighteenth century. During the American War of Independence, the privateer Paul Jones sailed in, pointed his guns at the town and said he would open fire if Fishguard did not pay 500 guineas in exchange for a local ship he had seized. Fishguard danced to the Paul Jones tune and paid up. In 1797 a band of Frenchmen scrambled ashore on the Pembrokeshire coast: the last invaders to land on British soil. But they were very drunk and rowdy and when a crowd of Fishguard women appeared, clutching pitchforks, they were at once demoralized and sensibly surrendered to the nearest army unit.

Like most out-on-a-limb people, Pembrokeshire folk are an independent lot. In the Gwaun valley, quite a remote district, the people still cling to the old calendar which is about a dozen days behind the one the rest of us have used for a couple of centuries. In fact, of course, they live by two calendars, the ancient and the modern, but they make a point of celebrating the eve of the new year on January the twelfth.

Pembrokeshire is like that in many ways: happy and a bit off-centre. In one sense it is two counties. The southern part, along with the Gower peninsula in Glamorgan, was settled by Normans and Flemings in the twelfth and thirteenth centuries, and the Welsh language was bulldozed out. There is a distinct, although inevitable, boundary across the county, called the Landsker, which divides Welsh-speaking Pembrokeshire from the English-speaking part, often referred to as little England beyond Wales. The Landsker runs from north of Haverfordwest, the county town, down to Laugharne in Carmarthenshire, and if you look at a map you will see that in the north of the county the place-names are Welsh and in the south they are English. The difference is also reflected in the education system: Welsh is taught widely in the north but hardly at all south of the Landsker. I have sometimes wondered why the English language in Pembrokeshire, surrounded by Welsh, was not eroded over the centuries in the same way that Welsh became eroded by English. Maybe the people were especially stubborn.

The first part of the Carmarthenshire coast I ever visited was Pendine. The name evokes the golden age of record breaking when the motor car was in its brash and exciting adolescence and those goggled, leather-helmeted drivers were the national heroes. You can drive your car along the five or six miles of hard sand, in the tyre tracks of those pre-war record breakers who, in the cramped and baking, oily, throbbing cockpits of their screaming cars, raced along beside the sea, pushing into the unknown for the sake of science, knowledge, excitement, glory and self-proof. There's a plaque beside the beach recording the five occasions between 1924 and 1927 when Malcolm Campbell and the Welsh ace J. G. Parry Thomas broke the world speed record here. I went down to Pendine the day that Parry Thomas's wrecked car was exhumed from the sand. Mourning villagers buried it there the day he was killed streaking along in pursuit of another record.

Thomas, a bachelor of forty-two, a brilliant engineer who was once the chief designer at Leyland's, broke the world record twice in 1926. In March 1927 he set out to beat Malcolm Campbell's new record of 175 miles an hour, set up a month earlier. His blue and white giant of a car, called *Babs*, powered by a twenty-seven litre engine, hurtled across the sand. It was close to the record speed when a driving chain burst through its guard and struck Thomas on the head, killing him at once. The local people dug a hole for the car and hid it away. Forty-two years later a college lecturer, anxious to restore it, had it dug up. One of the wheels was still intact and could be turned, and the fatal whip mark of the chain was still there on the cockpit.

If you mention Cardiff to people outside Wales they sometimes nod knowingly and say, ah, yes, Tiger Bay. But, as with some other parts of Wales, you should have been here yesterday. Tiger Bay in the old sense does not really exist any more. The area has changed and the people would prefer that you used the proper name for it: Bute Town. For Tiger Bay was a time as well as a place. As the teeming, cosmopolitan downtown district of Cardiff it had a reputation for life in the raw. There were pirates there, and fighting, drinking and whoring on the scale found in many dockland districts throughout the world. There was racial strife, too, of the kind we now see today, particularly in the United States. Bute Town, Tiger Bay that was, is still a mixture of accents and colours, but you don't hear of race trouble. The district is often held up as an example of a well-integrated multi-racial community, but there is an occasional expression of resentment that coloured people do not live or work in the centre of the city, but are kept to their side of the track.

Tiger Bay was Cardiff's Dodge City when the town was soaring on the dizzy thermal of the coal boom and the riches of the valleys were pouring in, as the drops of liquid slide into a bowl from the cuts in a rubber tree. Cardiff became the greatest coal port of the world and some of its tycoons made handsome fortunes. The chief citizens marked the prestige and wealth of their city by building, in Cathays Park, halls of government and culture, set among lawns and shrubs. This Welsh Washington has always given an extra swell of pride to all of the people of Wales, as well as to alberted aldermanic paunches.

Cardiff has been the capital of Wales since 1956, but was the capital by common consent for years before that. Nevertheless the official accolade was important to the Welsh people. To a nation divided to some extent by its geography, the capital is an institution providing a sense of focus and unity. Although towns more ancient, and more Welsh in character, like Caernarvon, Machynlleth and Aberystwyth, were put forward as better candidates for the role, Cardiff was the natural choice for a capital and the granting of the status was a recognition of Wales and the Welsh nation. While the coal valleys have declined Cardiff has grown steadily. It has cleaned most of the coal dirt from its fingernails and has become the major business and administrative centre. There is still an old rivalry between Cardiff and the valleys which radiate from it. When Cardiff looks back on its dizzy rise it says that it developed through the enterprise of its businessmen. 'On the backs of the miners, more like it,' say the valleys.

It's an understandable retort. In the valleys the people see that there is not so much coal moving out and down the line to Cardiff, but the drift of people is as steady as ever. Depopulation, eating at the life-fibre of the valleys, is a growing social problem. Of course, there is work being done to maintain the communities: factories are being built, ravaged land is being cleared, housing is being improved, and in some of the valley towns and villages this kind of work has really helped to keep up the special kind of vigour you find in these parts.

There are great plans for the Rhondda, for instance. There

is a vision of green valleys with a stable population, a Rhondda without coal mines.

The Rhondda, too, was a time as well as a place. And that single word, Rhondda, remains emotive. More than any other it rolls out a South Wales scene: yesterday's epoch of coal, pits and socialism, choirs and strikes, militant and weary men, bitterness and hard times. The time has gone. A great mixture of people lived, worked and suffered here through one of history's larger events. Men of big talent, leaders, poets, talkers, thinkers, orators, lived here. A unique society throve. A great deal of it has gone, but parts of the Rhondda remain impressive, with an abiding sense of history and a kind of battered dignity.

The Rhondda is a district of two deep, narrow, twisting and roughly parallel river valleys, each about ten miles long, which converge at Porth, sixteen miles from Cardiff. The northern-most valley and its brown river are called the Rhondda Fach— Little Rhondda—and the neighbouring valley is the Rhondda Fawr, the Big Rhondda, which contains the towns of Treorchi and Tonypandy.

The nature of the valleys and the positions of the pits created the characteristic housing pattern of the Rhondda: snaking terraces close to the pit heads, hugging the hillsides which were rapidly denuded and took on a more sombre aspect. Most of those houses which stand today were built between 1881 and 1914 to meet the needs of the swarming immigrants. The homes were of a standard type, built of local pennant sandstone, slate roofs, five-roomed and with small gardens or no garden at all. In 1871 the population of the Rhondda was 24,000. In 1923 it was 168,000—the peak—and, with more than 23,000 people to the square mile, was one of the most densely populated areas of the world.

At the start of this century more than half of the people in the Rhondda were Welsh-speakers, the chapel movement was all-powerful and the Rhondda settlements, which are like strings of beads beside the two rivers, had their separate character. Although their houses are tiny, most Rhondda people have always taken a pride in them. Scrubbed steps, shining doors and windows and a polished piano in the front room, if possible, have always been a part of the terraces of 'little palaces'. Today nearly eighty per cent of Rhondda houses are owner-occupied, one of the highest proportions in Britain.

The common enemies of degradation, hardship and misery moulded the varied people of the Rhondda into a great community which was marked by the qualities of loyalty and love of neighbour. The Rhondda story was one of enormous coal production, but the other side of the coin was bitter conflict, strikes, riots, explosions, devastation of the land, greed, cruelty. The indomitable Rhondda spirit survived all this and it was just as well that this spirit was forged, because after the meteoric rise of the Rhondda came the decline. The Royal Navy stopped burning coal and merchant ships, too, turned to oil. In the 1920s and 1930s the Rhondda, with all of South Wales and many other parts of Britain, suffered the bad times. The bottom dropped out of Rhondda's world.

At their home in Oxford Street in Maerdy, Sidney Warton and his wife, both nearing eighty, talked to me about the old days.

Maerdy is the end of the line, the last little township in the Rhondda Fach before the valley peters out in the foothills of the Brecon Beacons. Its name, like the names of some other towns in South Wales—Merthyr and Tonypandy for instance—is a bell that tolls back the twenties and thirties, the bitter years. And maybe the name of Maerdy lingers still in some faded and forgotten record in the Kremlin. For in the old days this small and drab town was known as Little Moscow.

When the hatred of the coal owners was at its fiercest, when the police were despised and children went barefoot and fathers went out in small bands to steal sheep, Communism had a heyday in Maerdy. Hardship united the people, the party meetings were packed, hundreds worked hard for the cause, and the cause was one of the great working class struggles. Arthur Horner, the lifelong rebel, miners' leader and a major figure in British Communism, lived in Maerdy at 93 Edward Street.

Mrs Warton has lived all of her seventy-eight years in Oxford Street, a straight, wide, clean street of neat terraced houses. When she married she simply moved her belongings across the street to her new home. In her parlour she talked about one of her sons, now dead. 'He was a brilliant boy. As a

141

youngster he went to Russia and it was all paid for by the Communist Party. In Moscow they showed him a map of South Wales and he saw that Maerdy was shaded purest red. That's how it was then. Red Rhondda.

'No wonder. I remember a Christmas dinner then. It was half a pig's head and cost a shilling and we thought ourselves lucky.'

Sidney Warton sits by the fireplace where, when he was in work, he used to have a tub in which he scrubbed off the pit dirt. He was secretary of the Communist Party in Maerdy for more than ten years and worked side by side with his hero, Arthur Horner. He went with him on the Welsh hunger march of 1927, which started in Maerdy, and recalls the incident, related in Horner's autobiography, when some of the marchers complained about the food. The cook became upset, particularly when someone called him a bastard, and refused to prepare any more meals. Horner, mediating, called the marchers together and demanded: 'Who called the cook a bastard?' Back shot a voice from the crowd: 'Who called the bastard a cook?'

Mr Warton said: 'There was a lot of tension between the police and the people of the Rhondda in those days. These Glamorgan police were well-hated and I'll tell you about an incident which says a lot about the relationship of the working people with the authorities. The miners' federation branch in Maerdy employed a sort of town crier at that time. He rang his bell on street corners and shouted out the union news and other bits and pieces. Sometimes he called out advertisements for the grocer. One day, in 1931, he sounded the alarm with his bell, saying that Bill Price's furniture was being taken away by the bailiff for non-payment of rates. You can imagine how, at the time, when there was hardly any work or money, such a pitiless action was bound to make the people angry. A big crowd gathered round the house but there was no trouble. Arthur Horner came up and had a talk with the bailiffs and they went away and the crowd dispersed. But then the police collared thirty-two of us and charged us with unlawful assembly. Arthur got fifteen months' hard labour and I got nine months. No wonder Maerdy was Red in those days. And people would have starved around here if it was not for the Communist Party. We held twopenny concerts and fed people with the proceeds. Yet, although they were bloody hard times my strongest memory is of the way the people pulled together. People didn't have much to give, but they gave help whenever it was needed. The community spirit then was something that glowed and kept you warm like a fire. All that has gone now, of course. We used to know pretty well every person in Maerdy and now we know hardly anybody. The old community spirit has disappeared and, if you ask me, Maerdy has gone to the dogs.'

I was reminded, when I went to an international archery championship in the Rhondda, that Welshmen long ago had a fearsome reputation as bowmen. They had discovered what others had not: that the long bow was a devastating weapon when it was drawn back so that the right hand was level with the ear. The best of all the Welsh bowmen were the men of Gwent—Monmouthshire—and they were the machine gunners of their day. Their fire power played an important part in Henry V's victories at Agincourt and Crécy; there is a record of them shooting arrows through a wooden gate four fingers thick and a story of a bowman whose arrow pierced a horseman's armour, thigh and saddle, and killed the horse.

Incidentally, the four hundred year argument about Monmouthshire—is it in England or in Wales?—has quite recently been terminated. Monmouthshire, for so long the envy of both sides and the property of neither, is in Wales, the principality's thirteenth county. The government wriggled out of the argument for years by using the halfway-house expression Wales-and-Monmouthshire. But that is out of date now and Welshmen who know and care about their history regard Monmouthshire's official 'return' as a wrong righted.

Up at the top of one of the Monmouthshire valleys a man told me about a tough old sheep which was so determined to get at his garden of vegetables that it lowered its head, charged the gate and burst through to the riches beyond. 'These bloody sheep, man. They're like locusts.' Another valley gardener said they were like gannets, another that they were like marauding Sioux. If you are in Wales in the spring you will see that it is a

143

land of lambs, as well as song. But in the valley communities close to the mountains you won't find much sentiment about lambs. The reason is that they grow into sheep and in these parts the sheep are hated.

The sheep, of course, are not so daft as they look. These are not the placid, woolly dumplings of picture book fame. They are mountain sheep, the guerillas of the sheep world. They wander into the valley towns like street corner toughs, thief-eyed and shifty, and rummage in the dustbins, blunder in front of the traffic and mercilessly level gardens and allotments. The tales of their feats of cunning and acrobatics and bare-faced cheek are legion. Every community has its share of sheep atrocity stories. 'Cunning? These sheep are almost human, man. If the walls are too high to jump over they will stand on each other's backs. And now they have learned a way of cross-ing cattle grids. They tuck their legs up under their bodies and, I swear this is true, they *roll* over the grid.'

Some local councils employ shepherds to round up and impound the strays and this has certainly mitigated the problem in some areas. But everyone agrees that a large-scale and expensive fencing policy would be the best answer. But the fences would have to be pretty high. Judging from what I was told, a South Wales sheep with the scent of the garden vege-tables strong in his nostrils becomes a sort of Pegasus with fleece.

I will end on a spiky note and give you an idea of what a valley gardener will do when roused. An old ram got into the habit of battering a garden gate near Merthyr, to get at the flowers and vegetables within. He would stand a dozen feet away and charge again and again until the fastenings broke. At last, the desperate gardener plotted revenge. He drove a number of six-inch nails through the gate so that they projected into the street. Then he covered his eyes as the ram charged for the last time.

# 10  A political expression

By the time of the General Election in June 1970, an era had all
but faded in Welsh politics. The coal field had dwindled, the
economy had become more diffused and the social scene had
correspondingly altered. The time when 240,000 miners were
in the pits had long vanished; now there were fewer than 40,000
miners and they no longer had the power to ensure that their
candidates got the seats in Parliament. The reign of the miners'
MPs, which had lasted more than forty years, was just about at
an end. The old guard, who were the contemporaries of Aneurin
Bevan, who were sent to Westminster by the coal valley communities and had been a part of the 'hard times' scene, were
giving way to the younger men who, better educated and
advantaged, were the product of the system and conditions the
older men had striven for. The legendary James Griffiths was
among seven Welsh Labour MPs who stood down before the
General Election to let the young men in. The new candidates
were lawyers and teachers and lecturers, so that there was, and
still is, a grumble to be heard over the pints of mild in the
miners' clubs about 'academics and intellectuals who haven't
been through the fire'. But most of the new men have their
roots in the industrial communities. Like their predecessors
they are sons of the valleys—and it probably wouldn't do at all
if they were otherwise.

It was not just the personalities that were changing, older
faces being replaced by younger ones. Although long-standing
and family political allegiance still counted for a lot, the pattern
of Labour's support was not what it had been. The changing
face of South Wales had inevitably led to a softening of loyalties,
a slackening of old ties, a challenging of Labour's political and
moral leadership. There were new forces at work.

For fifty years or so the Labour Party in Wales had been more
than just a political party: it was embedded in the fabric of life
in the valleys and was the massive and all-embracing political
force.

145

The roots had been laid down in the nineteenth century, before the Labour Party was formed, in the unique mining communities which mushroomed so rapidly in the spectacular coal-rush. Rhondda's population in 1861 was 4000; thirty years later it was nearly 130,000 and still growing. This new mass of people was not homogeneous, for the coal field attracted thousands of immigrants from many sources. In the decade 1871–81 half the people who moved into Glamorgan to work in the pits were from England.

The danger of the mining life, the hard times, the exploitation by the common enemy, steadily moulded the people into united communities in which loyalty, courage and care for others were the hallmarks.

At first, the fluid situation created by the inrush of labour raised many barriers to the formation of stable trade unions in Wales, and it was largely as a result of the work of English unionists that workers' associations with solid foundations were set up. From the ranks of the miners there emerged the majestic figure of Williams Abraham, known as Mabon, who was recognized as a leader of influence and authority. Like most working class leaders then he was a Liberal. In 1885, in the first election after the miners were given the vote, Mabon was elected MP for the Rhondda and, with candles in all the windows to light his triumphal way, was carried by jubilant miners up the valley to the chant of '*Mabon yw y dyn*'—'Mabon is the man'. In 1898 the small and autonomous district unions united to form the South Wales Miners' Federation, under Mabon's leadership. In the next twelve years the membership of the federation trebled to 140,000.

From the outset it was never a stuffy or remote union institution. It became closely involved with the social and domestic lives of the people in the mining communities and this grass-roots involvement was its bone and muscle. The first call on the pay packets in many thousands of valley homes was rent, sick fund and Miners' Federation. The 'Fed' developed into a great political and industrial force and militancy was central to it. Miners, families and union were fused into a single organism.

It was against this background that the Labour Party developed in Wales. At the turn of the century, the condition

146

of the economy was the dominant issue and the Liberals, the majority in Wales for more than thirty years, were uncertain and divided. Keir Hardie was elected Labour MP for Merthyr Tydfil in 1900, the first Labour MP in Britain, and this event marked the break between working class leaders and the Liberal Party. In the 1906 election six of the Welsh seats were held by Labour. Between 1906 and 1916 the Independent Labour Party held 20,000 meetings in South Wales. As the great class struggle between workers and capital developed, South Wales became known as 'the industrial storm centre of Britain'. The Labour Party's influence permeated steadily over the years— not like wildfire, for this was strong Liberal country. But, like chapel, pit and miners' lodge it became a part of the way of life. And after the First World War, when the Liberal grip was weak, the Labour men who spoke in the Commons were the authentic voice of the working people. By 1922 the majority of local councillors and Welsh MPs were Labour Party people. They expressed the aspirations and fears and anger of the mining communities and spoke for the men who were toughened by the hardest and dirtiest job in the world, men who honed political and social instinct and awareness in miners' hall classes and arguments, and in bitter fights with the coal owners.

In the twenties, unemployment, strikes, deprivation and disillusion, and a sense of betrayal, contributed to the great move away from Liberal allegiance. In the 1929 General Election twenty-five of the thirty-five Welsh MPs who were elected were members of the Labour Party. From that time on, Wales was a Labour stronghold. And at the end of the 1960s Labour held thirty-two of the thirty-six seats.

With English Conservatism rejected by the bulk of the Welsh people, the Labour Party's position in Wales looked unassailable. But during the 1950s and 1960s, Labour observed, with some uneasiness, the progress of a relatively new force in the political arena—*Plaid Cymru*, the Welsh Nationalist Party. In the early days few paid much attention to the nationalists; they were easily dismissed as an inward-looking minority, a crowd of romantics with nothing to offer the majority of the people. In the early days there was a strong strain of truth in the criticism. When it started, *Plaid Cymru*—which means party of Wales—was

not a political party in the generally accepted sense, not a
movement which sprang from the heart of industrial Wales, or
concern for the economy and the material condition of the
people. It was a movement with a romantic Celtic appeal,
which at first was a kind of debating society. It naturally
attracted teachers, writers, students and ministers of religion,
for it was—and is—very much concerned with the erosion of
Welsh qualities, with the decline of the native language, with
the retreat of people from the countryside, with the apparent
decay of national feeling, with the concept of Wales as a nation.
Its aim was to restore national awareness, to create a more
Welsh Wales with all the qualities that that term involves. Its
target has always been self-government for Wales, with
dominion status.

I said just now that *Plaid Cymru* was a new force. As a party of
substance it is certainly young. It was not until the 1959
General Election that it was able to put up twenty candidates.
But it was founded in 1925, at the National *Eisteddfod* at
Pwllheli, when the strands of several small nationalist groups
were woven together. And its roots go back to the nineteenth
century, to the arguments, writings and actions of a few ardent
nationalists. In the 1890s a Liberal-nationalist movement
burned brightly and one of its stars was Lloyd George. 'All our
demands', he once wrote, 'ought to be concentrated in one
great agitation for self-government.' But this movement, which
tried to promote an independent Welsh parliamentary party,
was uncertain and faded at the turn of the century. Probably, a
majority of the people of Wales were more interested in achieving a genuine equality with England, rather than home rule.
For the next generation it was the Liberal Party that was the
main channel for Welsh nationalist sentiment.

Nationalism itself, whether latent, emergent or flourishing,
has been a force in Welsh society and political life for a very
long time. The common language has not put an end to it, as
was once hoped. Conservatives have always tended to hope that
it would simply go away. The Liberal and Labour parties,
which have been very much more involved with Wales than
the Tories, have always recognized it as a force, albeit a rather
tidal one, and have, at various times in the past, promoted or

approved the ideal of self-government (or paid lip service to it when it was politically expedient).

In the past a number of Labour and Liberal politicians believed sincerely in home rule. Arthur Henderson, one of the builders of the modern Labour Party, once said that 'given self-government Wales might establish itself as a modern utopia'.

Nationalism, he said, meant the vigorous development of the material and moral resources of the people. 'It means a keener interest in the social, political and industrial problems which await solution. In my judgement, the Welsh nationalist movement has not yet fully faced its political and economic responsibilities. It is more concerned with the sentiment of nationality than with the practical concerns of Wales.'

The fact is, though, that the majority of those in the two big parties have not been impressed by self-government arguments and have been unionist at heart.

When *Plaid Cymru* was in its infancy the times were difficult ones in which to interest the bulk of the people of Wales—those who lived in the valleys of the south-east—in the decline of Wales and Welshness. The people wanted jobs, not dreams. Their vital political aim was to fight their way out of the indignities and deprivations of the coal field life and the long torment of unemployment. At that time men were stealing sheep from mountainsides to feed their families; the people wanted security, shoes for their children, a new deal. They chose socialism and it was through the Labour Party and, in many districts, the Communist Party, that people voiced their determination and anger. *Plaid Cymru* then was not a political organization and before the war many people had never heard of it. It was too young, too small and too poor to contemplate putting up parliamentary candidates in the mining valleys. It made its first appearance at a general election in 1929, in Caernarvonshire, and the candidate received 609 votes. 'The charge of the Light Brigade,' the nationalists said.

It took *Plaid Cymru* more than thirty years to establish strong grass roots, and more than forty years to emerge as a party with the essentials of worthwhile political action: firm and well-researched economic and industrial propositions rather than the stuff of dreams, an electoral organization, a permanent secretariat, a large number of publications and strong local groups—the component parts of credibility. By the late 1950s even its opponents could see that *Plaid Cymru* was developing into an organization of substance, offering an increasing threat to the status quo. It was chronically short of money—membership was five shillings a year and the fund was swelled by raffles. But in 1962 the party's ailing finances were given a lift when the writer and patriot D. J. Williams sold his family farmhouse, which he had immortalized in a book, and gave the proceeds of £2000 to his party. *Plaid Cymru*'s president, Gwynfor Evans, wrote: '. . . he gave every penny to the party, although he had little but his pension to live on. This handsome act did the party a power of good and can be seen now as a turning point in its fortunes.'

At each general election the party fielded more candidates. In 1955 it put up eleven and won 45,000 votes, in 1959 it fielded twenty and polled 77,000. In 1966 it again put up twenty, but received 16,000 votes fewer than in 1959. The other parties took comfort from this: it looked as if some of the steam had gone from nationalism. But fifteen weeks later came the rude shock of the by-election of Carmarthen.

This constituency was a fickle one and had pendulum'd between Liberals and Labour since the war. Lady Megan Lloyd George, a former Liberal, won the seat for Labour in 1957 and held it at the next three elections. In 1966, when she was seriously ill and could not go out campaigning, she had forty-six per cent of the poll. Gwynfor Evans, the nationalists' president since 1945, came second with sixteen per cent of the poll, more than seven thousand votes. Lady Megan died shortly after the election.

In the by-election campaigning, *Plaid Cymru* pulled out the stops. Also, it had as much television exposure as the other parties, something it does not get in general elections. Even so, on polling day a distinguished political journalist felt able, just before boarding his train to London, and before the count had taken place, to telephone his office with the opinion that 'Labour have it in the bag'.

The result, with Gwynfor Evans taking thirty-nine per cent

of the poll, and Labour coming second with thirty-three per cent, was a traumatic blow for Labour and for the Liberals. And, possibly, for the distinguished political journalist.

As Gwynfor Evans, first Welsh Nationalist MP, toured his constituency in the role of conquering hero, and was then welcomed by an ecstatic crowd and flapping Red Dragons as he reached Paddington on the way to the House of Commons, the Labour Party was dismissing the result as a freak, a protest vote and not a positive one, an electoral indulgence.

There can be no single explanation for the *Plaid Cymru* success at Carmarthen. The party put it down to its great growth during the sixties, to a steadily growing feeling in Wales of rejection of London government policies. The element of the protest vote was certainly there, although in the fifteen weeks since the General Election little had happened that was of electoral significance. The severe economic measures and the collapse of the national plan were then in the future. I think that the electors of Carmarthen were annoyed with the Labour Party for allowing Lady Megan, a very seriously ill candidate, to stand in the General Election. There was, in any case, a flood tide of nationalist feeling as well as the solid core of traditional nationalist voters. Television was clearly an important factor; Gwynfor Evans emerged as the most outstanding candidate and, on polling day, there was a mood of 'Let's vote for good old Gwynfor'.

The Carmarthen by-election conferred considerable credibility on *Plaid Cymru*. Nine months later, a by-election in Rhondda West, one of the safest of Labour seats and right in the heartland and spiritual centre of Labour-in-Wales, turned out to be something of a sensation. The nationalist candidate came within 3306 votes of taking the seat. And in 1968, at the Caerphilly by-election, the nationalist reduced Labour's majority from more than 21,000 to under 2000.

'Now we are really on the menu,' the nationalists were saying. And, indeed, they were heady days for *Plaid Cymru*. Membership of the party grew to more than 40,000 and the leaders stressed that theirs was the largest party in Wales.

The nationalists' strong threat, their ability to split the vote (to Labour's disadvantage in particular), and the changing textures of the political scene, made Wales a separate arena in the 1970 General Election. *Plaid Cymru* rightly regarded the election as a crucial test of credibility, a time to make a big push. More money than ever before was put into the campaign and, for the first time, the party fought in all constituencies. The optimists were talking of holding Carmarthen and gaining another seat, or even two, as well as sweeping up 200,000 votes. The more hard-headed knew that general elections always change the political environment in favour of the two major parties and that the Labour candidate had only to pick up 2000 or so votes to topple the *Plaid Cymru* leader from his Carmarthen seat. They also knew that Labour's election machinery was, to say the least, powerful, experienced, well-organized.

A Labour organizer explained: 'The people of Wales are radical and want a socialist government. A Tory government is anathema to the great majority. And when they vote nationalist at by-elections they are satisfying their radical spirit and the need to protest. We all understand that. But they only vote nationalist when it is safe to do so—that is, when Labour is generally doing well. When it comes to a general election most people recognize a choice of two. They vote for a government of Britain.'

In Carmarthen a Labour campaign worker paused to say: 'Gwynfor Evans is a splendid man and in some parts of Wales he has almost reached the point of being canonized. But he will be out this time because it is a general election.'

This confidence was rewarded. The *Plaid Cymru* chief was unseated and nationalist hopes were dented. But there was encouragement elsewhere. No seats, but they polled a record of nearly 176,000 votes—more than eleven per cent of the poll—compared with 61,000 in 1966. The party was now the second force in six Welsh constituencies. It had almost trebled its vote compared with 1966 and this was not achieved merely by contesting all the seats instead of twenty. On average, the vote in these twenty seats was almost doubled.

*Plaid Cymru*, like the Scottish National Party, complained bitterly about the allocation of time for party political broadcasts; it is a long-standing source of grievance. The nationalists have always maintained that air time should be allocated on the basis of seats contested by parties in Wales and Scotland. A few months before the election the nationalist parties sent a joint memorandum to this effect to the leaders of the three major parties. The 'carve up' of air time by the big three was, the nationalists said, unfair and a danger to democracy. In another attack on the air time share-out *Plaid Cymru* said there was 'a despicable attempt to stifle the emergence of new political thought'. During the election campaign a nationalist criticism on this subject was related to a Labour minister. 'If they want equal time on the telly then they'll bloody well have to fight all 630 seats,' he said.

Labour's relief at removing the nationalist thorn at Carmarthen was certainly offset by other aspects of the election (quite apart from the unexpectedness of defeat). There was a drop in the turnout in Wales—always high in such a politically-minded country—and Labour polled its lowest number of votes since 1945. The Conservatives' proportional share of the poll was lower than in any election since 1950 although they won seven of the Welsh seats, equal to their record of 1959. The results proved that the election in Wales had a separate quality. Alongside the turnout factor, *Plaid Cymru*'s big push was a major cause of damage to Labour's position and certainly questioned the future security of seats once believed absolutely safe.

There were also two curious and unhappy situations for Labour. In Pembrokeshire the former Labour MP Mr Desmond Donnelly stood as a Democrat and the seat passed to the Tories. (Mr Donnelly founded the Democratic Party in 1969, a year after his expulsion from the Labour Party, and after nineteen years as the county's MP. His quarrel with Labour divided loyalties in the county. He eventually joined the Conservatives.) At Merthyr Tydfil, Mr S. O. Davies, the constituency's MP since 1934, had been asked by the local party to stand down. It was felt that he was too old to carry on. He was then eighty-four —tall, snowy haired, distinguished in his familiar black jacket, pinstriped trousers and black boots. He had been a fighter, a rebel, and sometimes an outsider, all his life. He was one of the last of the old miners' MPs. He went into the pits at twelve, taught himself English and educated himself at home and in evening classes, and remembers casting his first vote for Keir Hardie.The constituency party had hoped he would agree to a graceful bowing-out, with the usual dinner, orations, honours and thanks due to a man with a lifetime of service to his community. But he would not hear of it. He was stubborn and stood as an Independent Labour MP candidate against the official Labour man. He was expected to be crushed. But he won. His victory, by more than 7000 votes, was a painful kick for the Labour Party and, on the day after the election, there was, all over South Wales, a great eating of hats. (Mr Davies died in February 1972.)

On that day Gwynfor Evans was taking his defeat philosophically enough. 'A blow, yes. But a check, not a disaster. I've no doubt there are people saying this is the end for the nationalists. They have been saying that since we started. I have been in this movement for thirty-six years. When I started there was only a handful of us. Now there are 40,000 members.'

Gwynfor Evans has had two major ambitions in his life: to raise a family in the old Welsh manner and to see Welsh nationalism grow so that Wales can achieve self-government. He has fulfilled the first. An English-speaker by upbringing, he learned Welsh as an adult (and recently wrote an acclaimed history of Wales in Welsh), trained as a lawyer and returned to the family home of Llangadog, beneath the slopes of the Black Mountain in Carmarthenshire, to run a market garden, raise a family and work for nationalism. His children are Alcwyn, Dafydd, Meleri, Guto, Meinir, Branwen and Rhys, loyal and home-loving and unimpressed by city fleshpots.

As for the second ambition—well, it is clear now that the majority of the Welsh people want a greater say in the running of their own affairs, some kind of elected assembly. But there is not yet a mass movement towards the ultimate devolution of self-government. The atmosphere in which Welsh nationalism is now alive and growing may change unpredictably. The movement, as it grows increasingly mature, may go from strength to strength. But the subject is too full of imponderables for worthwhile forecasting. *Plaid Cymru*'s leader, however, is convinced that nationalism will not stop advancing now and that some form of self-government, leading to full self-government, is not far off.

The party's profile has changed considerably in the past ten years or so. It is tougher, more professional, better organized. The poets and writers are balanced by the economists, lawyers and trade-unionists. It has always attracted the young people, the Welsh-speakers, the country people and the lecturers and ministers, and it attracts them still. It has had growing support from the middle class people, English-speakers and those working class people who, disenchanted with the economic policies of the Labour Party, and quite unable to bring themselves to support the Conservatives, are attracted to radical nationalism. A considerable part of *Plaid Cymru*'s support, perhaps half, comes from English-speakers—the party's chairman, Dr Phil Williams, is not a Welsh-speaker—and the membership has grown fairly steadily in anglicized areas.

The party is no longer the mere 'crowd of writers and airy romantics' of earlier years. Which is not to say that it has no writers and poets; it has many. And a certain kind of romance is a part of the appeal. But the idealism now has the backbone of ideas, proposals and arguments which are supported by research. A hundred researchers, for example, spent three years drawing up *Plaid Cymru*'s economic plan for Wales, and a team of lawyers, including a QC, spent more than a year working on the party's proposals for a Welsh constitution. Both these documents were submitted to the Crowther commission on the constitution, to support the case for self-government.

As a political organization the party is much harder than it was even a few years ago and its growth, and the change in the pattern of its membership, has led to changes of emphasis in its actions. It is strongly cultural-nationalist, concerned for the language, but it has to balance these considerations with a demand from many of its supporters for professional, credible economic ideas, and good answers to hard questions. Along with the language it has to think of unemployment. It has to make clear that its ideas on self-government have been worked out and it seeks, not separation, but confederation, a partnership with England. One of the most common of the anti-nationalist epithets is 'separatist'. Hissed down a microphone at a public meeting it develops quite a chilling ring and evokes a Wales with a frontier and customs posts, cut off from Britain.

In Welsh politics there is a special passion and sometimes a bitterness not usually found in England. The arguments and knockabout that are part of politics are usually conducted on a more abrasive and emotional level in Wales and there is not the same inclination to compromise, to practise what is called the art of the possible. There is more directness too. Not so much sitting on the fence. In Welsh politics a man is expected to make up his mind and declare where he stands. Welshmen take their politics seriously; it is in the blood.

In this kind of environment the Labour Party's resentment of nationalist successes has been particularly sharp. And understandably. For Labour's position in Wales for the past half century has been that of the party of the status quo. And when this newcomer, this small nationalist party, started to grow and to complicate matters, particularly in those few constituencies where the Conservatives were strong, it naturally felt stung and hostile.

There was also a growing conflict within the party. Labour's leadership in Wales, a leadership in ideals as well as in politics, has enabled some of its members to express their Welshness, their concern for Wales, through the party. They have not wished to go the whole nationalist hog by any means, but they have felt able to work for Labour action on such matters as devolution and the sensitive issue of greater recognition of the Welsh language. But Labour in Wales is also, of course, a part of the British Labour Party machine and many of its members are glad to feel themselves a part of this central, broader movement. They have decided to be British first and Welsh second. As one of them explained to me: 'Wales is simply a piece of a larger unit and very dependent upon it. As socialists we are internationally minded, looking at the wider scene.' In this section of the Welsh Labour Party there is not much sympathy for the idea of a great measure of devolution, not much time for matters like the language. The party has been seen to be divided in its attitude to Welshness, to be inflexible, and this is regarded by some of its supporters as one of its failures.

The conflict of loyalties has led to some great internal wranglings over, for instance, devolution (Labour decided, after much heart searching and in-fighting to back an elected council for Wales), and the touchy language question (again there was much argument before the party agreed to support the idea of bilingual road signs). And there were rows over the content of the Welsh Labour Party's bilingual magazine *Radical* which ran for ten issues in 1970–1 and was then closed down. 'Too much neo-nationalism in it,' growled one Labour man. 'People who feel like that should get out and join *Plaid Cymru.*'

Welsh nationalism is attacked as narrow, introspective, petty and parochial. It is always criticized on these grounds by those who believe there is virtue only in the frying of bigger fish. The nationalists, so concerned with what is happening in their own garden, are regarded as essentially tiresome. Nationalists themselves say it all depends on what is meant by parochialism and quote Aneurin Bevan's dictum: 'If you are going to plan the world you must first of all control that part of it that you will want to fit into the whole.' Wales is certainly a small country, but many are smaller, and with almost two and three-quarter million people and a sizeable industrial stake, it is a fair-sized parish. Moreover, the nationalists say, their nationalism does not stop them having an international outlook.

*Plaid Cymru* is socialist, decentralist, community-minded, pacifist. People are attracted to it for a variety of reasons. They have come to believe that *Plaid Cymru* is now a more radical party than Labour, that Labour in Wales is now too London-Socialist and too little Welsh-Socialist; they have become dissatisfied with Labour's performance in mitigating the economic ills of Wales, or they feel that Welsh nationalism is the best political expression of identity with the concept of Wales as a nation. That, however, is not to say that everyone who feels Welsh is a nationalist. Indeed, a considerable number of people who feel Welsh reject nationalism: they regard it as arid.

There is another important reason why people find that *Plaid Cymru*'s philosophy coincides with their own beliefs. In this kind of nationalism, as in the struggle for the Welsh language, there is a strong element of people versus bigness. It is a revolt against the crushing uniformities of late twentieth century life, a struggle for independence in the broadest sense against big government, big business, big bureaucracy, big units. It is a belief that the dignity of man is greater in a decentralized order than a centralized one. It is not happening only in Wales, of course. The feeling manifests itself throughout the world in a variety of guises.

Gwynfor Evans sees his movement as very much a part of this wider context. 'All over the world there is a change in attitudes. Sensitive people are rebelling against the pressures of a technological and mechanical society. They are against its impersonality and inhumanity. They feel that their humanity and dignity is being degraded.

'So you have this shift to a more humane society in which people can create their own conditions and environment. People are being manipulated by the big forces in life and the world has grown more complex and terrifying. There is a vacuum because of the decay of religious belief. People are not sure now where they belong in terms of time and eternity. They want security.

'Most people have this need to belong. When they are uprooted and pushed around they become a proletariat. Our work is against the proletariatizing of our people. Increasingly, people feel the need for what Wales has to give them: a pattern of values they can rely on, a recognition of an individual's-worth.'

Saunders Lewis, the architect of modern Welsh nationalism, a founder member and first president of *Plaid Cymru*, withdrew from active politics more than twenty-five years ago, but from time to time makes an important contribution to political debate in Wales, and never shrinks from criticism of the nationalist party. He told me: 'Nationalism has made considerable progress in forty-five years, but not always the progress I would like to have seen. So much of nationalist propaganda is dictated by the desire to establish a nationalist party, *Plaid Cymru*. And so the party tends to compete with English parties, particularly the Labour Party, and especially in such matters as promising to tackle unemployment, promising to introduce new industry and creating a higher standard of living.

'Really none of these things has anything to do with the fundamentals of nationalism. A great deal of the voting at general elections and by-elections is a protest against failures of English government, and not an assertion that there is, here, something that ought to be preserved for the sake of its civilization. 'That is the only real reason for nationalism, you see. That there is something that ought to be preserved.'

At the heart of Saunders Lewis's concept of Welsh nationalism is his distinction between independence and freedom. Independence for Wales, he maintains, is not essential, but freedom is, and within this freedom the Welsh people have the responsibility for their social and cultural life.

'With the freedom to be responsible we could shape the fundamentals in the life of our own people. The matter of independence, of being separate, is another thing altogether. It involves sovereignty and the problem of defence. These seem to me to be irrelevant in the concept of this freedom to be responsible. They are not necessary to nationalism. There is a certain amount of political separation, a very minimal amount, essential for creating this unity of our nation. Some form of Welsh parliament is necessary. But I never have thought that the concept implied complete political separation.

'Suppose we had a utopia—suppose we had an English government which was as anxious to preserve the whole Welsh tradition as any Welshman. What point would there be in having a Welsh government? An English government which would help Wales would remove the basis of some of the nationalist vote. But we are a human community and it is impossible for Englishmen to feel for the Welsh tradition and for Welsh civilization and the unity of the Welsh people. It is impossible for them to feel it or to regard it as important: no nation ever understood another nation.

'As I see it, Welsh nationalism is inevitably and essentially a minority movement. Whether it will become politically important enough to have a great influence on administration and government, I do not know. But even as a minority movement it has influence in slowing the drift into an impersonal and depersonalized civilization. So that I would say its value for the whole of Welsh life is immeasurable.

'With a nationalist movement there ought not to be a party political view at all. *Plaid Cymru* is not a political party like English political parties; it can never be so. It offers itself as the spearpoint of a nation, a nation in subjection. Welsh nationalism is essentially a movement to restore self-respect to the Welsh, not the respect of outsiders.'

Nationalist parties tend to be judged by the actions of extremist nationalists. Outrages in the name of nationalism are gifts to the enemies of the philosophy. In Wales, the period of the bombs in the 1960s, and the trouble surrounding the investiture of the Prince of Wales, damaged *Plaid Cymru* to some extent because 'these nationalists' were condemned for the trouble and some people were persuaded that nationalists were a headstrong and dangerous lot. To win friends and influence people *Plaid Cymru* needs to show itself as a responsible party of some substance. It has to demonstrate that it has a gradualist philosophy and has to emphasize its moderation. It has to indicate that it is one segment of the nationalist movement, that it is not the whole and is not, therefore, the host for all the small groups that have nationalist ideals.

The great majority of people prefer respectability and are suspicious of blazing zeal. *Plaid Cymru* has always condemned violence and insisted on the constitutional path. 'That's the trouble with *Plaid Cymru*,' a man said to me, with some disappointment in his voice. 'Too damn respectable. Needs some fire in its belly. Let's be honest now—the English government only takes a bit of notice when the agitation is strong and there's a bomb under a pipeline.'

It is a difficult situation at times. Within the nationalist party there is a close identification with, and strong support for, the cause of the Welsh language. But there is also concern that the well-publicized direct-action activities of the Welsh Language Society are crystallizing social tensions and threatening to hurt the party.

Indeed, Gwynfor Evans said a year after the 1970 General Election that the militant campaigns of the language society had contributed to the loss of his seat. He, of course, is desperately concerned for the language. Among many of the younger people there is a belief that the nationalist party should fit the Saunders Lewis concept of it and concentrate on the language issue. They maintain that it is the language society that now has the 'pure' role that *Plaid Cymru* had when it was in its infancy, before it was a political force.

During the next few years the agitation for more devolution of London-based power to Wales will increase. The Labour Party, the Liberals, the nationalists, and many of the individuals who gave evidence to the Crowther Commission on the Constitution, all asked for some form of elected assembly for Wales. During 1971 an opinion survey carried out on behalf of the commission showed that only ten per cent of the people want the system of government in Wales left as it is. And while only ten per cent of the people want Wales to assume total responsibility for its government, two-thirds want a system which would allow as many decisions as possible to be taken in Wales. Most people in Wales, I think, are in favour of what they call 'a greater say'—although there are varied and sometimes rather vague views about how this could be achieved.

During the autumn of 1971 two reports on the Welsh economy were published, which added fresh fuel, a rather smoky fuel as it turned out, to the endless debate about the viability of Wales in a self-governing situation.

The nationalist party has always maintained that self-governing Wales could pay its way. The party's best economists, and a research team of a hundred people, produced an impressive document in 1970 showing how it could be achieved. The Labour and Conservative parties hold that the notion is preposterous. Everyone, however, drew comfort from the statistics published in the two reports. *Plaid Cymru*'s newspaper declared: 'Social accounts prove free Wales is viable.' While Mr George Thomas, Secretary of State for Wales in the Labour Government, said: 'The figures knock on the head the old nonsense that Wales could run itself.'

Neither side could hope to prove conclusively from the statistics that a self-governing Wales could, or could not, manage. The argument goes beyond budgets and figure-juggling hypotheses; so much depends on various decisions and, as with the Common Market, the only genuine test perhaps is to jump and find out. The argument is, at heart, a political one.

Whether devolution on a large scale will come is a question that throws up some complex problems. For one thing the position of the Welsh Office and of the Secretary of State for Wales, in a situation where there is an elected Welsh assembly, must be considered. The creation of the post of Secretary of State in 1964 was an important event for Wales. The idea was by no means new: Keir Hardie called for such an appointment in 1910. Colony-minded Whitehall probably thought him an eccentric fellow for making such a suggestion.

The post is a Cabinet one and the holder of it is the political head of a large department of State, the Welsh Office. Within a few years the Welsh Office has become successfully rooted in the pattern of Welsh life. Indeed, many people wonder how on earth they got along without it. Appeals, protests, requests, petitions, and all the other aspects of public dealing with government, go naturally to the Welsh Office, not to remote London. This success of the Welsh Office is not surprising: it demonstrates that Welsh people like decisions on Welsh matters made in Wales.

In a lecture in September of 1970, Mr Ted Rowlands, a former Under-Secretary at the Welsh Office, said that the department had become a significant political pressure group in the British government system. The Secretary of State had become a Welsh ombudsman and one of the department's most significant successes was in ensuring that the voice of Wales was heard more distinctly in the Cabinet and in Whitehall.

Mr Rowlands instanced two important occasions when the Welsh Office took up Welsh causes at top level. In the first, the Secretary of State fought against British Rail's decision to close the central Wales railway and persuaded Cabinet colleagues to reject the Ministry of Transport's case for closure. In the case of the proposal to drown the Dulas valley in mid-Wales (see page 106), the Secretary of State was involved in a political battle to uphold the findings of the inspector who conducted the public inquiry. He argued that defeat would destroy Welsh Office political credibility. The Secretary for the Environment conceded the political point and the Dulas valley was spared. It was just as well. The uproar that would have followed an adverse decision would have been enormous.

For all this, the influence of the Welsh Office on national policy is weak, Mr Rowlands said. Some strategies are drawn up without consultation with the Department for Wales. 'Whole areas of major policy profoundly affecting Wales have been determined within Whitehall with a negligible contribution from the Secretary of State's office.'

One answer to this, it is argued, would be to give the Welsh Office a larger and more positive function, with an adequate intelligence and economic department and more independence in handling financial resources. But the counter-argument is that a greater measure of administrative devolution would carry a danger of government by civil service: there would be more bureaucracy but not so much democracy. The answer to that, it is said, is an elected assembly to which the Welsh Office would be accountable. But Mr Rowlands says the implications are enormous. 'Any elected council will have to discover functions in relation to the activities of central government administration in Wales and would make superfluous the post of Secretary of State for Wales as it has developed over the past seven years. There would seem to be little or no room for an elected council, the Secretary of State and the Welsh Office as presently constituted. An elected council will inevitably challenge the whole system of the accountability of Welsh Office administration to Westminster and Whitehall.'

Devolution, the future government of Wales, takes up an increasingly large part of political debate in Wales. But the basic issues of economic health and unemployment are still the most important ones. Wales has been for more than forty years in need of government help as a development area and in some parts the spectre of the old days of unemployment flits through minds. As far as one can tell, the bulk of the people will continue to make their political expression through the Labour Party.

Both the Labour Party and the nationalists say that the people of Wales reject Conservatism, although we must not forget that the Conservatives have seven Welsh seats, and the nationalists say that in the coming years the struggle will be between *Plaid Cymru* and Labour. That is certainly true in some constituencies.

But *Plaid Cymru* is still having to work towards the goal of substantial credibility, the vital and mysterious factor of political existence. It has many talented men and women working for it, but it does not yet have at its centre a body of men of large experience in politics and administration. Nevertheless

163

nationalism will continue to grow. In their contribution to the book *Celtic Nationalism*, Gwynfor Evans and Ioan Rhys wrote: 'In 1925, the word nationalist still savoured of liberalism and democracy and self-determination, so much so that official Liberal candidates in Wales had sometimes described themselves as "Welsh Nationalists". During the thirties, however, Franco, Hitler and Mussolini made nationalist a dirty word and later still it has become associated with apartheid in South Africa. Neither has the trouble in Ireland been good for the nationalist image. . . . It has been something of a tragedy for Wales that fascists and imperialists and racialists should virtually have taken over the word nationalist by the time *Plaid Cymru* has begun to campaign to any purpose. . . . We shall go on calling ourselves nationalists until the word has recovered its former repute.' Nationalists in Wales have gone a long way towards achieving that aim.

Wales is by long tradition a country of the left. The outlook is a part of the national psyche. It grew under the policies of the Tudors which set out to make Wales and England equal, but succeeded only in making most Welshmen feel resentful and a dominated minority. Out of this grew the dissent and radicalism which were honed in the great class struggle, first through the Liberal Party, then through the Labour movement.

*Plaid Cymru* is likely to go on growing and strengthening its base because Wales is a natural catchment area for the protest vote, because more people in Wales are experiencing a disenchantment with British socialism, because nationalism has a considerable attraction for young people and because the Labour Party is not certain how to grasp the nettle of Welshness.

As far as one can tell, and speculation is unrewarding, political nationalism will remain a minority movement in the foreseeable future. Nevertheless, nationalism is a root feature of Welsh life. The nationalist party is tiresome to its enemies—how could it be anything else?—because it keeps on talking about Wales. It has created, inside and outside Wales, a much greater recognition of the Welsh identity. It has forced successive governments in London, and some of those London politicians of anti-provincial views, to have a greater awareness of Welsh needs than they might otherwise have had.

# 11 'Where toil the Cymry'

In the northern parts of Wales the people used to have a saying: *'Lawr i'r gweithiau yn y de.'* It meant: 'Gone down to the works in South Wales.' Sometimes, said with a shake of the head or a knowing smile, it meant that a man had had to hurry away to hide in some narrow street in the teeming and booming valleys of the coal field because he was in social hot water . . . a small crime, a fight, or a girl in the family way.

It also meant that a man had packed up to find work and a better standard of living for his family in the Rhondda. It was a resigned commentary on the migration of thousands of people from the rural areas of north and mid-Wales to the industrialized south.

Those nineteenth-century families who piled all their belongings and their hopes into wagons and trains, and left for ever the hard life of rural Cardiganshire, Merioneth and elsewhere, to take part in the great industrial explosion, were committing themselves to the hardship of the mining life. Few of their descendants, however, are going into the pits. They are working in the light industries, manufacturing plants, offices, factories and service industries of the south. And they are also leaving the country altogether. For the sombre fact is that emigration is a tradition and is still a facet of the Welsh scene. The economic situation persuades many people to follow a path that has been well-beaten by scores of thousands of Welsh people—the path to England and beyond. Young men and women are still 'going down to the works in South Wales' but many others, when they pack their bags, are not moving from one part of Wales to another. They are quitting.

Wales today is a country whose economic and industrial structure is undergoing a dramatic and desperately important transformation. The process is not without considerable pain and is by no means nearing completion.

It is the aftermath of the age when coal was all, the number one employer, and iron and steel were in the supporting roles, and there was not much else for a boy seeking work save the town hall, the Co-op and the blessed and prestigious security of the Post Office. The fight in Wales, being carried on by government agencies and the hard-working Development Corporation for Wales, is to develop a core of growth, to strengthen and diversify the industrial base by development and subsidy, to persuade industrialists and entrepreneurs to bring work to Wales.

The economic problem is enormous and is veined with sensitive cultural, social and political problems. The continuing seepage of young life and talent from rural Wales towards the industrialized south-eastern part of the country, and to England, is having an effect on the delicate and vulnerable quality of Welshness. As Wales sloughs the old skin many Welshmen wonder how much of immense value will be lost.

The story of the coal industry is the largest part of the story of South Wales. It is one of the great human stories of all time. The people here have had the traumatic mass experience of the dizzy rise of coal, its tormented heyday and the agony of its long and bitter decline. Coal has left its indelible mark on the Welsh soul, as it has left the unmistakable blue scars on the hands of the miners.

Some of those communities which grew up and throve around the pits in the valleys now have but dull prospects of a reasonable future life. A number have grown thin, old and tired. When mining goes a lot goes with it. The drain of the people out of the valleys, down to the land of relative plenty along the coastal belt, seems impossible to stop. The young people, in particular, have to be realistic: they cannot afford to be sentimental. But the story is by no means all gloom. Many towns have been working hard to come to terms with the industrial and social changes.

Aberdare, in Glamorgan, is a good example of a former coal town that fought to re-establish itself as its economic strength crumbled and its people drifted away. Before the depression there were more than twenty pits around Aberdare, and more than 20,000 miners working in them and living in tight grey rows of cottages. The town had 50,000 people, a team in the Football League, and the proud nickname of *Brenhines y bryniau,* the Queen of the Hills. Then the slump squeezed the people out. They packed up and left Wales for ever, for the Midlands and the South-East, sitting on the furniture in the back of the vans to save the rail fare. At the depth of the depression half the men of Aberdare were unemployed. Diversify or die: the writing was plainly on the wall, and not just for Aberdare. Then, in 1938, a group of businessmen founded Aberdare Cables, bought twenty-four acres of land and started production in a new factory. It showed what could and should be done to fill the holes left by decay. Gradually, more factories were built near the town and, to a large extent, industrial expansion absorbed men as the coal mines closed one by one. In 1965 Fforchaman colliery was closed, the last man stepped from the pit cage, and Aberdare's century of marriage to coal was over. The town has made a successful transition from a mining community to a community earning its living from a variety of sources. There are more than fifty firms based in the district and the town has a large stake in engineering and electronics. The transition has not been painless—unemployment figures indicate a need for more development—but what might so easily have become a town with its heart eaten out has become a town of bustle and purpose. The winding gear of an old colliery in the town is a reminder of the past, but Aberdare is not looking back.

In the past twenty years the coal industry has been shedding men as a tree sheds leaves in an autumn gale. Although it has declined it remains a big business by any standard and will be so for a long time: a vital industry in South Wales and in the national context. Yet, in the 1950s and 1960s, mining's future looked desperately bleak to many of the men working in it. The industry was shrinking—and squeezing out its men by the thousand. Many miners, not old, but too old, have found themselves facing a future with little prospect of work. When the coal mines were nationalized in 1947 there were more than 200 pits working in South Wales and 114,000 men working in them. And when the first nationalized pit was axed—a pit at Gwaun-cae-Gurwen in the Swansea valley—the reporters were there in force to record the anger and bewilderment. After that, though, closures became commonplace enough, averaging seven every year, and the column inches on the subject grew less. Today there are fifty pits in South Wales and 38,000 miners.

The sixties, in particular, were years when the contraction of mining was severely felt. At the start of the decade there were more than 100,000 people working in the industry. At the end of it there were 40,000. Incredibly, the once-mighty Rhondda has just two collieries left and there is a plan to keep one set of pit head machinery as a museum piece. By the end of the century the mining industry in South Wales is likely to settle to between thirty and forty mines extracting the best anthracite and dry steam coal in the world.

For more than twenty years the coal mines had their ritual funerals: the Coal Board announced that a pit was losing money and would be closed if it did not become more productive. The pit was put on the 'jeopardy list'—that is, the miners were faced with a choice of having to increase output considerably or see the pit closed. Difficult geological conditions, absenteeism and a lack of confidence were the miners' enemies and, during the sixties, there was a vicious circle of absenteeism, loss of heart, loss of production, more absenteeism and closed pits. In many worn-out pits the jeopardy list was usually the last formality before close-down. But in some pits the men made a fight of it; some tough managers and natural leaders with large personalities took up the challenge and worked to inspire the men to push up productivity to the required level in the given time. If they succeeded there was champagne and their picture in the paper. If they didn't, the wheel stopped turning.

When the pit cage of a closing mine reached the surface for the last time, the men who stepped out, blinking in the sunshine, felt that the writing on the wall had been re-emphasized. For them there could be no future in coal mining. They felt a part of the depressing cycle of closures and loss of confidence. By 1970 mining had become an industry of middle-aged men.

Outside the colliery at Blaengwynfi, in Glamorgan, the day before it was closed down, an old miner told me that in the year before closure the 400 men in the pit had doubled the output. But the Coal Board had decided that it was still not a worthwhile pit because of geological problems. 'The young men feel disheartened,' the miner said. 'They are quitting the industry—and who can blame them? Within an hour's travelling of Blaengwynfi there is secure and better-paid work in the factories. On the surface and in the fresh air.'

Many ex-miners settled without regrets into jobs in the new factories attracted to Wales by the government's development area incentives. But many mining men had reservations about some of the factory jobs that were offered and snorted with contempt about tough miners going to work in 'dolls' eyes factories'. By the end of 1970, however, the rush out of mining had gone too far for the Coal Board's comfort. There was a shortage of manpower and a particular shortage of new entrants, the school-leavers who would be the industry's future strength.

The board launched a big advertising push to get back those miners who had left, and to interest school leavers in a mining career. The advertising, on television and cinema screens, in newspapers and in leaflets dropped through tens of thousands of letter boxes, stressed that mining in the seventies had something positive to offer, that the bad days were over. It also underlined the masculine aspect of mining. Coal mining, after all, is one of the last 'man's world' strongholds and the advertising made the point that it was a man's life in the mines—'Join the men in mining'. The publicity drive paid off. In the first three months of 1971, for example, more than 1600 men joined the industry in South Wales and more than 1100 of them were former miners returning. They came back because the economic situation meant there were not so many factory jobs, because they missed the allowance of free coal which is one of the miners' perks, because the pay was better—and because they had missed the mining life.

Some may scoff at the idea, but most miners appreciate that working underground has a special quality. Julian Kinor, a repairer at Bedwas colliery in Monmouthshire, became fed up with mining when morale in the coalfield was low and decided to get a job 'outside'. He worked for five months in a tea factory. 'But I couldn't stand it,' he told me. 'People outside are different. They think of themselves too much. Frankly, I missed the comradeship and unselfishness of men who work underground. A man has no dignity pushing buttons at a factory bench. In the mines we work as a team and have pride in our team. And, to be honest, I like getting the concessionary fuel for my central heating. Coal mining is certainly hard and dirty and there is always an element of danger. But responsibility counts and most men like responsibility.'

Between nationalization and 1971 the Coal Board invested more than £220 million in South Wales pits, £10 million a year. And at the end of 1971 a board official was able to tell me that mining was no longer an industry with a miserable face.

He was enthusiastic. 'The investment is paying off. We are a profitable industry and a very worthwhile one. Those who shook their heads a few years ago and said we would be finished off by oil and nuclear power have been proved wrong. Our coal is needed and we can sell every ton we dig out of the ground. In one year wastage and absenteeism have dropped sharply and productivity has increased. In 1970 we closed down only two pits in Wales, the lowest total since 1950. In future only the exhausted and completely uneconomic pits will be closed.

'Mining is a much more attractive job today. The pick and shovel days have gone and mines are highly mechanized. Miners are technicians who are kept up to date with new developments and their pay and prospects are better. When a new coal face is being opened up the men who will work on it attend a teach-in so that they are completely involved in the development. Coal mining in South Wales is more stable today than it has been for twenty years. It can offer security and it has the kind of prestige it has not known for many years.'

If, after two decades of agonizing contraction, coal mining in Wales is at last achieving stability, there is every reason to be thankful. When there is an endless struggle to put more bone and muscle and flexibility into the economy of a development region, an important labour-intensive business like mining is a valuable asset.

For nearly forty years Wales has been a development area, an area in need of help, where various economic carrots and sticks have been tried with varying results. The fact that Wales has for so long been a development area indicates how hard the struggle is.

The problem is that Wales has no long-standing centre of

growth in its economy. With coal in retreat, with the mighty steelworks, too, having to adapt to modern technology and challenges and thin out their work forces, Wales had needed, still needs, a constant transfusion of new industries and aid. Those areas of England which forge ahead without much trouble are prospering because they have sound traditional growth centres which expand and give birth to more growth with great ease. They get jam on their bread and butter without asking for it. Wales, like other regions which are development areas, suffers through being in a peripheral situation. It has an inadequate road system, although this is gradually being improved. It has too many branch offices and factories for its own health: when firms have to economize it is the branches they lop off first.

The well-being of the Welsh economy depends, naturally enough, on the well-being of the British economy as a whole. But it is not as simple as that. When British economic fortunes are rising, Wales does not have a *pro rata* increase; it achieves a lower level and booming Britain does not mean, necessarily, booming Wales. But should there be a wane in the level of the economy overall, the effect of it is nearly always magnified in Wales. Unless the British economy has a fairly high level of prosperity, and growth seeps from the English boom areas, the policy of inducement cannot be completely effective.

At the heart of the Welsh problem is the requirement that the productive structure be transformed to the extent that Wales does considerably better than the overall British economy— which must itself be vigorous and rising. It is a tall order.

It is no wonder that, bearing in mind the critical problems of Wales, many Welshmen are concerned about the principality's prospects in the Common Market. They believe that as Wales has suffered economically because of its geographical fringe situation it must suffer more severely because it is relatively more peripheral in the European context. They have always resented the remoteness of London government and are concerned about being part of a system in which, they believe, the remoteness will be intensified. They feel that without the basic equipment of a sound economic structure, a much-improved road system and the right kind of support policy, Wales is badly placed to take advantage of Common Market benefits and that the first few years of Market membership will be a hard time to Wales; in fact, they fear a marked economic decline in Wales. There is concern, too, at the effect on Welsh farming, largely hill sheep and dairy farming. Many people in Wales therefore feel sceptical and resentful and, above all, vulnerable. Some look beyond the economic effects and foresee damage to the quality of Welshness, the culture and the way of life. They believe these will suffer largely through an acceleration of depopulation.

But, of course, there are others in Wales who feel that all these fears are exaggerated, that there will be a proportional share for Wales in the general growth, that Wales will benefit through being an integral part of Britain. They think that even if the short-term effect of Market membership will be adverse, the long-term effect will be beneficial. Moreover, they believe the government will be forced to devise a much better policy for tackling the problems of depressed areas.

Certainly the need for a more positive regional policy cannot be denied. It is overdue. In the early 1970s rising unemployment and the continued emigration of Welsh people have brought the shadow of the thirties flitting into people's minds.

Michael Foot, MP for Ebbw Vale, has said that in the valleys there is 'an intelligent fear' that the wheel may be turning full circle. Neil Kinnock, MP for Bedwellty, in Monmouthshire, described the fears in a Commons debate in 1971:

'We have a new generation of workers in South Wales who since the war have become accustomed to a level of relatively high employment and to secure jobs and fairly advanced affluence—people who expect to take holidays every year and to have comfortable homes equipped with all the modern conveniences and motor cars. But this generation is now experiencing something it has never known before. These people who undertook new skills and have secure occupations, at the age of thirty to thirty-five, are now knowing the sickening worry their parents' generation knew. Whereas thirty years ago the workers in South Wales were almost wholly engaged in the mines and the steel works, they are now employed as textile workers, engineers, chemical workers, glass workers and in all the other diversified trades that have developed since the war,

and they are coming to know the worry, insecurity and desperation that was a permanent feature of the life of the pre-war
generations. Behind every redundant worker there are another
two worrying themselves into distraction about who will be
next—sweating that every weekend the management will put a
slip into their pay packet, or a notice on the board.

'A whole generation bred on security now experiences the
threat of the axe over their jobs. This kind of situation is
nothing short of disaster. It is disappointing in human terms,
and it must cause everyone in this House the greatest frustration. But frustration, compassion, sorrow and regard for the
position of these people are not enough. We want positive
action. The government must change their regional jobs policy.
There is no alternative.'

The 1971 census revealed that the percentage population
increase of Wales lagged considerably behind England's (0·30
per cent compared with 0·54 per cent) and that the drift away
from rural Wales continued at a disturbing rate. Five of the
thirteen Welsh counties were shown by the census to have lost
population, as well as many of the South Wales valleys.

In the fifties and sixties the population of South Wales
increased at only half the United Kingdom rate and in the
three years up to the summer of 1969 the number of people in
work fell by almost 50,000.

The effect of that is naturally felt throughout the community;
it is 50,000 fewer wage packets being spent in the shops.

The Welsh word for depopulation is *diboblogi*. It has a sad
ring to it because it conveys a strong sense of loss. Between the
wars, half a million people, a fifth of the population, left the
slopes and valleys—and not until 1961 did the population of
Wales grow to equal the 1921 figure.

Depopulation is a particularly serious problem in mid-Wales,
the heartland of beautiful and rugged country. For twenty
years people have been drifting out of this area at the rate of 700
a year, a serious loss considering the population is only 175,000.
Depopulation is a sickness that still threatens to make large
parts of mid-Wales economically arid.

There are signs, however, that two organizations which have
been trying to stem the outward flow are beginning to achieve

some success. Government investment, factories, new jobs and new houses are beginning to slow the rate of depopulation. Gloomy hand-wringing about the loss of young talent is now being replaced, in some areas, by talk of growth.

During the 1950s, people in this conservative part of Wales began to realize that only development of the right kind would prevent mid-Wales becoming a social and economic desert. In 1957 Merioneth, Cardiganshire, Montgomeryshire, Breconshire and Radnorshire set up a development association to attack the problem. Since then, sixty factories providing 3000 jobs have been attracted to the area. Future growth will be centred on the towns of Aberystwyth, Bala, Brecon, Llandrindod Wells, Rhayader, Newtown and Welshpool which will be the job-centres of the region.

An important part of the effort to make mid-Wales a worthwhile area for young people and their families is the development of Newtown, an amiable market town on the upper Severn, as the first new country town in Britain. The intention is to double the population to 11,000 by the early 1980s. Houses and factories are going up and the advertisements aimed at attracting new blood to Newtown have the flavour of the Australian government's emigration publicity. The message is about an area 'on the move' where there is plenty of room to breathe.

'We believe we are offering a better life,' I was told by Peter Garbett-Edwards, secretary of the mid-Wales and the Newtown development bodies. 'At a time when big towns are overcrowded and there is more concern about the quality of life, we are providing opportunities for life in a small, active and very congenial country town, a life in beautiful surroundings.

'Fighting depopulation is absolutely vital. The outward migration had been emptying the heart of Wales and making the north and south grow further apart. Encouraging growth in this region not only makes it better off economically. It helps to make Wales more united.'

The economic struggle in Wales will remain an uphill one as far as one can see. 'Nevertheless, a good deal has been achieved,' an official of the Department of Trade and Industry told me. 'There are setbacks, of course, disappointments, bad years, but

174

overall the story is one of a continuing growth and improvement.'

Diversification has removed much of the old dread in South Wales of dependence on one or two basic industries. The Welsh industrial base has certainly diversified on a large scale since the war, rather too much in the eyes of some economists who regard diversification for its own sake as something of a weakness, partly because of the 'branch factory factor'. Two thousand manufacturing organizations are now employing a third of the working population of 980,000, and almost sixty per cent of the people are in the service trades. The steel industry has traditional and strong roots in Wales; South Wales is one of the world's most important steel manufacturing centres and the enormous complex at Port Talbot, more than four miles in length, and newly equipped with an ore terminal, is one of the largest steelworks in Europe. Recent reorganization and a huge investment programme—British Steel's stake in Wales is more than £400 million—have rooted the industry even more securely here. Its fortunes in the coming years, in the competitive world steel market, will be closely watched in Wales.

There was a time when people were content enough to read that new factories were creating more jobs in Wales. Now there is more concern with the type of job, a realization that the prime test for a new industrial development is not necessarily the number of jobs it will provide. Wales is looking for a richer employment spectrum, and the importance of science-based industries like petro-chemicals and plastics is better appreciated. South Wales needs more of this type of industry, located, preferably, in growth centres. There is a need, also, for a force of skilled local people working in the front line of technological advance—and for a better intelligence service to provide the information on which economic plans can be based.

One of the great industries of Wales is tourism. In 1970 it earned £108 million in the principality, fifteen per cent better than in the previous record year, the golden year of the investiture, 1969. Eight and a half million people spent a holiday in Wales in 1970 and 10 per cent of them were Welsh people. Tourism spreads the money around Wales more evenly than some industries, which channel their proceeds over the border, and, naturally, there are frequent calls on the tourist board and other organizations to increase and improve hotel accommodation, caravan parks and other facilities. Well, no doubt all of these things are necessary, but some parts of Wales in the high summer are over-populated with tourists and stuffed with caravans so that there is a danger that people destroy the very qualities they come to enjoy. Great beauty and peace are perhaps the prime attractions of Wales and, to maintain them, balances have to be struck.

Tourism helps many people in rural Wales no end. Some farmers say a caravan parked in a field for a while is worth a cow or two. And more than one farmer has bought a caravan so that he and his family can live in it while the paying guests get away from it all in the whitewashed farmhouse and sleep in the farmer's bed. Over-dependence on tourism is unhealthy for a community but, to some extent, *gwely a brecwast*, bed and breakfast, for English tourists is helping in the fight against *diboblogi*.

# 12 The return of the squirrel

More than anything else, it was the cruel tragedy of Aberfan which made the people of South Wales look with a sense of outrage at the industrial defecations of the coal owners, at the dirt, rubble and the black Fujiyamas of colliery spoil which are truer memorials than statues and portraits. Until the morning of 21 October 1966, when one hundred and sixteen school-children and twenty-eight adults were engulfed and killed in the collapse of the mountain of thick wet slurry, most of the people of the mining valleys had simply put up with the coal tips and dereliction, hardly thinking about them, accepting them as the inevitable and permanent by-product of industrial endeavour. There were some exceptions, but in the main the people, the local authorities and the government were apathetic.

After the first shock wave of Aberfan, public rage was jerked and channelled into a desire to erase, clean or at least reshape the blackened wastelands. Within a month of the disaster the Secretary of State for Wales established in the Welsh Office a small department quite unlike any other Civil Service depart-ment: the derelict land unit. It had no special powers and it could not compel anyone to do anything about derelict land and hideous tips. But, by acting as a kind of flying squad, by harnessing the public mood, by drumbeating, assisting, advis-ing, sometimes cajoling, it has stimulated land reclamation on a scale that would have been thought impossible a few years ago. The unit accepts growled comments about 'bloody evangelists' as a grudging admiration.

Without giving any room for complacency—there is a lot of work ahead and a lot of money is needed to do it—the story of land reclamation in Wales since 1966 is an example and an inspiration. By the early 1980s, if the enthusiasm and momentum are maintained, most of the industrial scars in the valleys should have been eliminated. The land reclaimers, largely the local councils, are painstakingly painting the valleys green again.

Between 1960 and 1967 only four local authority reclamation schemes, covering ninety-nine acres, and costing £33,000, were carried out in Wales. But a study of dereliction in the lower Swansea valley, started in 1961, and a derelict land panel set up by the former Welsh Economic Council in 1965, pointed the way to future progress. The 1966 Industrial Development Act provided the framework for reclamation by setting up a system of grant aid for local authorities wanting to rehabilitate damaged land. Councils normally get an 85 per cent grant on a scheme, plus rate support grant in many cases. Thus when the tip fell upon Aberfan the legislation was already there to provide the means for tackling the ugliness in the Welsh valleys. The disaster provided the dreadful lesson and, therefore, the will. An early survey charted 19,000 acres of Wales in the derelict land category but a more thorough mapping project now under way is expected to show that the true figure is much nearer 30,000 acres.

In the five years after Aberfan the derelict land unit approved nearly 130 schemes, covering more than 3000 acres. These cost more than £6 million and more than £4½ million were paid out by the government in the form of grants. The great majority of the schemes have been undertaken by local authorities, in the Welsh tradition of community action. The number of schemes has increased year by year and this trend will continue. The disused collieries are being turned into factory estates, spoil heaps are being removed or flattened to make room for a clinic or a school, gigantic tips are being levelled, moulded and planted to blend with their surroundings. The government departments have shown a fairly liberal approach to reclamation: although the rule is that cleared land must contribute towards the industrial development of a district, the principle is now well established that pure amenity schemes which aim to make an ugly piece of land relatively attractive can be grant-aided in the normal way because a site-seeking industrialist is impressed by the overall appearance of an area.

John Price, administrator of the derelict land unit, who was born near Aberfan, told me: 'We certainly have a sense of purpose in this department; we want to get rid of these awful industrial scars and messes on the face of Wales. The old attitudes of apathy have vanished and throughout Wales there's a great determination to clear up the bad land and a confidence that big things will be achieved. In this unit we have adopted a rather aggressive attitude from the start. We have always moved out of the office and into the valleys to provide a service of advice, to draw up plans, give rough estimates. We have been seen to be caring. We have always wanted to spend the money available and we have cut red tape. The local authorities have taken up the challenge.'

In Monmouthshire the county council and ten local authorities, whose areas encompass the major part of industrial dereliction in the county, united to form their own land reclamation group. Their reclamation officer, Alun Rogers, has a healthy hatred of the black scars in the once-lovely valleys. 'My job is to turn the clock back a hundred years or so,' he said, as we watched giant earth-moving machines devouring an evil old tip.

The first scheme under the auspices of the Welsh Office derelict land unit was undertaken by Cwmaman council at the small village of Glanaman in Carmarthenshire. Here, for more than fifty years, a black monster of a coal tip, the Gelliceidrym tip, had overshadowed the village and, at about the time of Aberfan, it began to move and threaten the houses which lay at its foot. Because it was potentially dangerous it was clearly a priority and the bulldozers moved in. Gelliceidrym became a gentle and benign hill, planted with grass and trees.

'The nicest thing,' a villager told me, 'apart from the fact that the tip no longer comes into my back garden, is that we get the sunshine much sooner in the morning and in the chapel we have the light of the sun streaming through the window, something we haven't experienced in half a lifetime. The shadow has been lifted and it's worth that bit extra on the rates.'

The bit extra on the rates amounts to just over one new penny a year over thirty years. The council gets only £250 from a penny rate and the Gelliceidrym scheme cost £150,000, but after the 85 per cent Welsh Office grant, and rate support on the balance, the council was left with a bill of only about £7500—and it was money well spent.

The industrialization and scarring started at the end of the eighteenth century when the developing factories of England demanded an increasing supply of iron. There were ironstone outcroppings in the belt of land from Merthyr to Blaenavon and ironworks were founded. The woodcutters moved into the nearby forests to fell the trees to make the charcoal to smelt the iron ore. The destruction of the fair country of South Wales had begun. When the trees had gone the ironmasters dug out coal by open cast methods and soon the naked slopes were pitted with holes and spoil heaps. The onset of the steam age brought an increased demand for coal which outstripped the demand for it as the basic fuel in iron and steel making.

In the nineteenth century the growth of the mining industry continued the denudation of woodlands—the timber was needed for pit props—and the heaps of waste from the mines grew up on the mountainsides. The first rubbish from the Merthyr Vale colliery was dumped on the mountainside above Aberfan more than 100 years before the disaster.

In the village of Gilfach Goch, a few miles from the Rhondda, men really kicked beauty in the teeth. Here Richard Llewellyn set his best-selling novel *How Green Was My Valley*, an epic of social struggle and industrial greed. The village's pretty Welsh name, which means 'little red creek', became a bitter joke. The coal years left it a worn-out, depressed and ugly little gulch. Coal mining began here in 1812 and eleven mines cast out the slurry and rubbish for vile black tips; the last pit closed in the early sixties and Gilfach Goch was, within a few years, a decaying community of 2700 people, a community physically and socially bombed-out and very much in need of help.

In 1971 Glamorgan County Council set up its own derelict land team and cast around for a suitable first project. Not for long. Gilfach Goch was a fairly obvious choice. A two-year programme of restoration costing £200,000 was started in September 1971. The local people were enthusiastic. The project included the shaping and planting of tips, clearing up of heaps of shale and rotting industrial junk, tree-planting, the making of footpaths, the cleaning of dirty streams and improvement of houses. 'I can hardly believe it,' an old man said. 'They say that when it's all finished people will want to build new houses and will come to live here because it will be so nice.' The name of Gilfach Goch was on a list in the derelict land unit office, headed 'The Dirty Dozen'. As the bulldozers moved to start the clearing work, the name was ticked off.

For all the dereliction, there is still a great deal of fragile beauty in the valley country: South Wales is usually misrepresented as total black country. But you may be driving though a brutally damaged part, then turn a corner and find an unexpected corner of loveliness that has survived the brutality. Inevitably I have become a little defensive about the landscape of South Wales: I used to think, before I saw it, that it was all raped countryside, but the surprise and the reality is that a great deal of it is beautiful and I enjoy showing it to newcomers so that they may enjoy the same surprise and revision of preconceptions. It does not always work like that. Sometimes I will drive a newcomer into the valleys, but the mist will hide all the pleasant country and lift only to reveal a glimpse of a shattered valley, coal tip, broken pit gear and all, and the passenger nods with a kind of satisfaction. 'Just how I imagined South Wales would be. Bloody awful.'

Hard to believe today, when the mist is swirling around and the rain makes the slates of the terraces gleam, and the industrial junk looks especially dismal, that the Rhondda district was once so beautiful that it was described, years ago, as 'the gem of Glamorgan'. People here still like to tell strangers that once a squirrel could have travelled from tree to tree all the way from the head of the Rhondda to Cardiff. When squirrels frolicked undisturbed, the Rhondda was green, secret and romantic. Its fast little streams worked the wheels of the pandys, the mills where cloth was woven. But beneath the steep and wooded slopes of the valleys were the best seams of steam coal anywhere in the world. The exploitation of them was to be a tremendous industrial and social explosion. In 1849 George Insole started mining at Cymmer and the industrialization of the area began. In 1851, when Wales was represented at the Great Exhibition by a few lumps of coal, an important seam was discovered at Cwm Saerbren and, with the hunger of the steam age to meet, the Rhondda was, within a few years, the centre of an unprecedented coal rush. It became the most intensively mined area in the world, ruthlessly exploited for the industries of Britain, for the world market, for the insatiable boilers of the Royal Navy and the merchant ships. There was an array of mines, one every few hundred yards in some parts.

Today there are just two coalmines left in the Rhondda, one in each valley. The decline, to those who remember this district's tormented heyday, has been as amazing as its rise. The great gaunt pubs, where miners washed away aches and coal dust with pints of mild, are boarded up. The isolated pubs on the hillsides, built close to the pits, where men would gulp a tot before going underground, are empty. And everywhere there is the debris of the rush to wring the coal from the ground. Rotting machinery, derelict buildings, unlovely acres of waste ground, rubbish and dirty water.To make matters worse the local authority for years pruned the trees with an enthusiasm that amounted to brutality. Above all there are the tips, cones and whaleback heaps of waste slurry from a century of coal mining.

For people who have been in the Rhondda a lifetime, who lived, worked and fought in it when it was the prime coal centre, and watched the spoil heaps steadily rise and spread, plans being made now for the Rhondda of the future are hard to take in.

The scheme for the Rhondda of 2001, which is being worked out in discussions between the people and the local authority, envisages these battered valleys without a coal mine—'Rhondda without a coal mine. Now that's something for old folk to think on,' an old miner said—parklands, green grass coats for reclaimed land, conifer forests and clear streams, and one pithead winding gear and one tip left standing . . . as museum pieces.

The consultants who prepared the Rhondda valleys development plans wrote that 'although the patient may be sick, he is far from incurable. Study and analysis have uncovered social problems, physical decay, economic blight and environment insensitivity that must be righted. Nevertheless we are dealing with an environment which is physically beautiful and full of possibilities. . . . Central government has recently affirmed that the valleys will not be allowed to die. . . . Nevertheless we found a community still reeling from the cataclysmic change which has overtaken it within the past thirty years. Stripped of its living, threatened by new towns and communities, by-passed by life-giving arteries of communication it is little wonder that the remaining population looks with some suspicion and cynicism at planners and regional and central government. We believe this phase has now ended.'

There will have to be a lot of work, a lot of faith and a lot of money—more than £90 million—to create this future Rhondda. The aim is to make the district a worthwhile place for young people to settle in, to stabilize the declining population at about 80,000, to build new factories, homes and schools, clear up the derelict land, and yet retain the sense of the past and the character on the grand scale which is part of the Rhondda.

Up at the top of the Rhondda Fach, in Maerdy, a woman of eighty said: 'We saw the tips growing and we took them and all the mess that mining made for granted. We didn't look at our surroundings so much then. It was politics, the bosses, the hardship and getting enough to eat that was on our minds then. All this environment business today—well, it's marvellous and I'd like to see the hills green and all the mess cleared up. But it's really for the young people and the children. I come from the old Rhondda. It was a piece of history, something we lived through and no amount of grass and tidying up can alter that.'

The Rhondda development plan says that the future appearance of the Rhondda will be radically affected by the activities of the Forestry Commission. It paints this picture of a sylvan Rhondda of the future. . . . 'Out of 24,000 acres in the borough [of Rhondda] as many as 15,000 may be ultimately afforested if the smaller farms cease operations. . . . The Forestry Commission plans to use a variety of species, including hardwoods, to avoid the dull effect of large areas of single species. . . . As well as changing the micro-climate of certain areas the change from moorland to forest will affect bird life and increase the variety of species in the area. The range of small mammals will widen and in time there is the prospect of deer as well as polecat and pine marten colonizing the plantations; the broad leafed woods will provide the richest habitat of all.'

The day when the squirrel could swing from tree to tree down from the Rhondda to Cardiff has long gone. But in a comparatively few years an adventurous trapezing squirrel will be able to cover a fair amount of ground along Rhondda's tree-clad slopes. To have mentioned such a possibility, even a few years ago, would have brought a short and disbelieving laugh. There is still much to do, but today in valleys, once black, the people can talk of the green grass of home.

# 13 Wales for ever

In a bar at Dolgellau, chief town of lovely and hard-up Merioneth, the subject was that endlessly worked-over, endlessly new one—Wales. 'Of course we have an inferiority complex,' my companion said. 'What would you expect? The people of Wales have spent 500 years looking up England's backside and seeing the sun shine out of it. But things are beginning to change now. Our skins are a bit thicker and we tend to flex our muscles a bit more as a people and we are more self-confident.

'Sometimes, when the talk gets around to the Welsh way of life, which is basically a pattern of rural life in Welsh language communities, people say: "Ah, you should have been around yesterday." They feel that a lot of good qualities about the old days have vanished and have not been replaced by anything better. Well, one of the sad things about yesterday was that hardly anyone was fighting for the language, or worrying about depopulation. People say Wales for Ever, but what does it mean? What are the chances of survival for a Wales with its own character and language? Without those things Wales will be just a geographic term. And look at what is happening to our country; look at what is happening to Merioneth for instance. The young people are going away and the holidaymakers and the elderly people from Merseyside and the Midlands are moving in. They aren't interested in Wales, they aren't interested in who we are and they don't want to know about the things that concern us. They can't understand the feeling we have about Wales. To them it's just a pretty province to play in. Have you been to some of the little places, once Welsh? Wolverhampton-by-bloody-sea, some of them.

'Well, it's the Welsh people who are selling off their cottages for good money, and you cannot blame them for being human; it is not just a Welsh complaint, though—the cottage buyer from the town is altering the character of rural life everywhere. And who can blame the town and city people for wanting to escape? The tragedy here is that the character of rural Wales is so fragile and precious. And many of the English people are unreasonable.

'They start complaining when some awful American show is dropped from the TV schedule to be replaced by a Welsh programme, and they moan about their kids having to learn Welsh, as if in some way they are being infected. If they went to live in France or Germany would they complain about the language of the television programmes? Wouldn't they expect their kids to learn a little French and German?

'You can do something about the pollution in the rivers and on the land in Wales, but you can't do anything about the people-pollution. Look at what is happening to bits of the Spanish seaside, and along the Mediterranean coast: full of English people demanding fish and chips and cups of tea and all the things that are just like home; sniggering if they see someone trying out his broken Spanish. That's what I mean by people-pollution, an appalling uniformity.

'Do I sound like a snob? A chauvinist? A Welsh fanatic? I suppose I do. But I can't help it. I feel frustrated when I see what is happening to Wales. I get worried when I see that the kids have precious little Welsh language television to look at, and plenty of American junk. I know that a lot of television is inevitably rubbish but I just wish it could be Welsh rubbish instead of English and American rubbish.

'I see the kids seduced from their Welsh heritage and the Welshness rushing out of Wales like blood from deep cuts.'

It is natural enough for sensitive people who are aware of their Welshness and of what might be termed the Welsh condition, to rail against the forces that are sapping the strengths and distinctive qualities of Wales, to wonder what Wales and the Welsh will be like in the next century, to wonder if Welsh Wales can survive. Some have a dread vision of a future Wales without its distinctive birthmark and soul.

In this nightmare the enemy is *seisnigrwydd*, which means anglicization, but sounds much more sinister. It does not mean that Welshmen who are anxious to advance the Welsh language despise English or Englishmen. The few who say they do are not at all typical. It simply means they have a strong belief in their own identity and the patch of the planet they have made their own. English happens to be the vehicle which carries the threat to their heritage.

It is important, I think, to view what is happening in Wales today in a national and international context because it is, to a considerable extent, a part of a larger pattern.

The modern emphasis on economic growth, on centralization, on increasingly large corporations and bureaucracies, and the inclination to examine human endeavour in terms of profit and usefulness, tend to push individual and community needs and feelings into the background. The pursuit of a perfection of efficiency, the speed of the new industrial revolution, the execution of lame ducks, the remoteness of administrators and the apparent worship of bigness, have led to a situation where respect for people and their dignity has been lessened. There is a dehumanizing process going on. Our well-meaning politicians, our administrators, our architects with their heartless tower blocks, all of us, are taking part in processes which tend to make us conform and ignore the fact that people are warm, clumsy, vulnerable, sensitive individuals. It should not be surprising that people rebel. For the forces of what we might call the system are threatening individual and community values. The assertion that people count is the link between such varied groups as Third London Airport protesters, London motorway fighters, people campaigning to keep country schools and cottage hospitals open, preservationists of all kinds, and Welsh language campaigners. It is the way of things that such people get labelled as extremists. Demonstrations are criticized, but there is developing among our politicians and civil servants a somewhat cynical belief that people do not mean what they say until they are blocking roads and struggling with policemen.

The conflict between people and the system has heightened the awareness of roots and community. In the past decade there has grown a new awareness of the quality of Welshness, a new confidence and a willingness to assert it. Elsewhere there has been a greater awareness of being, say, Scottish, Basque, or black. 'Welsh—and proud of it' is the equivalent of 'Black is beautiful'.

The language struggle in Wales, and the growth of national awareness, have made more Welshmen think about Welshness.

It is quite irrelevant to argue that Welsh-speakers 'can all speak English anyway'. This is a common expression but it evades the issue. People supporting the struggle to secure Welsh wish to save the fundamental manifestation of their nationality, the embodiment of the spirit and history of a unique community. In historical terms this struggle is inevitable. It would be unrealistic to expect culturally aware people to stand by, inactive, while the soul of their nationality and community slips into the quicksand.

In an address to the Honourable Society of Cymmrodorion in 1968, the late Professor Charles Gittins, a distinguished educationist, a Welshman who did not speak Welsh, discussed the language question:

'The outlook for the Welsh language is clearly a matter for deep concern because here is a crisis which has to be faced by this generation. In such a serious situation, it is immensely important that the majority of Welshmen, who speak only one language, should be reminded that language is much more than a means of communication. Language gives colour to experience, embodies feelings, gives an edge and a sensitivity to relationships. Language enshrines folk memories . . . gives to the individual a feeling of belonging, an identity which nothing else can replace.

'Everyone in Wales who feels the value of our bilingual heritage should realize that time is desperately short. If we are to create a wider and more general bilingual society, we must appeal to those who have acquired hostile prejudices against the language while very young, to re-examine them and to ask themselves whether they are not the victims of a conditioning process which stems from nothing more than the mere accident of the place in which they were born.

'It may be that many more Welshmen will quickly come to see, as I am sure our grandsons and those who come after them will certainly see, that great value is to be attached to the difference which the possession of a language assures.

'The trend in Western civilization is to uniformity. The curse that awaits the coming generations is that everyone will look the same, talk in the same manner and have the same interests and activities. When such a fate dawns, the human spirit will react and will ask not for affluence, but for identity, for difference, particularly cultural difference. If this opportunity is to be afforded to those who come immediately after us, a heavy responsibility falls upon this generation to work for a renaissance of the language, a reversal of prejudices and a pride in what we are.'

The struggle for the Welsh language is a minority's struggle for existence within its own life-design. Because the relationship between the English-speakers and Welsh-speakers will, in the long run, be the decisive factor, the issue is how far a minority can go in pursuing its dream of a bilingual society, in persuading the public to agree, in persuading the authorities to bend and to comply with the spirit of the law, without undermining a basic goodwill that has so far outweighed enmity and bigotry.

Among some Welsh-speakers there is now an edge of desperation and, among some English-speakers, a bristling of resentment. The ingredients for a harmful split in Welsh society are certainly there, and backlash has been predicted. At the time I am writing, however, there has been no violent or serious manifestation of either.

The advancement of the Welsh language is an eminently worthwhile cause and I believe that the fight going on for it may have begun just in time. Britain will be a poorer place if we cannot afford a little room, time, money, protection and tolerance for the language which, for more than fifteen centuries, has answered for this civilized and enchanting corner of the earth.

# Book list

*Artists in Wales*, essays. *Gwasg Gomer*, Llandysul, 1972.

J. C. Banks. *Federal Britain?* Harrap, 1971.

George Borrow. *Wild Wales*. Collins, 1862.

*The Historical Basis of Welsh Nationalism*, lectures. *Plaid Cymru*, 1950.

Glyn Jones. *The Dragon Has Two Tongues*. Dent, 1968.

Goronwy J. Jones. *Wales and the Quest for Peace*. University of Wales Press, 1969.

Gwilym Arthur Jones. *Owain Glyndwr*. University of Wales Press, 1962.

R. M. Jones. *Highlights in Welsh Literature: Talks with a Prince*. Christopher Davies, Llandybie, 1969.

*The Legal Status of the Welsh Language*, a report. HMSO, 1965.

Robyn Lewis. *Second Class Citizen. Gwasg Gomer*, Llandysul, 1969.

*The Mabinogion*. Dent, 1906.

Gerald Morgan. *The Dragon's Tongue*. Triskel Press, 1966.

Kenneth O. Morgan. *David Lloyd George*. University of Wales Press, 1964.

Prys Morgan. *Background to Wales*. Christopher Davies, Llandybie, 1968.

*Report on the Welsh-speaking Population*. HMSO, 1962.

*The Shell Guide to Wales.*

Ned Thomas. *The Welsh Extremist*. Gollancz, 1971.

*The Welsh Language Today*, a report. HMSO, 1963.

David Williams. *A History of Modern Wales*. John Murray, 1950.

# Index

Aberdare, 166–7
Aberfan tip disaster, 2, 118, 127–8, 177–8, 180
Abergele, bomb explosion at, 115, 119–20, 121
Aberystwyth, 54, 90, 91, 128–30, 139, 174; University of Wales, 129–30; national library, 130
Abraham, Williams (Mabon), 146
*Academi Gymreig*, 74
accents, 5
Alders, Frederick 118–19, 120, 121
Anglesey, Welsh teaching in, 65
Anglo-Celtic Watch Company, 33
anthem, national, 7, 90
archery, 143
Arnold, Matthew, 55, 79
*awdl* (verse form), 41

Bala, 174
*Baner ac Amserau Cymru*, 72, 98
Bangor, 1971 national *eisteddfod* at, 41, 96
bardic names, 40
BBC Wales, 41, 56, 60; Welsh language programmes on, 69–71; Saunders Lewis's lecture on (1962), 73, 79–82
Beasley, Mr and Mrs Trefor, 83
Bevan, Aneurin, 157
Bible, translation into Welsh, 16, 52
Biblical names, 32
bilingual education project, 61–3, 65–6
bilingual road signs, campaign for, 86, 89–91, 94–6, 98–9, 157
Blaengwynfi colliery, 168
bomb outrages, 102, 106, 109–22, 160
Borrow, George, 49
Brecon, 128, 174
British Steel, 175
broadcasting—*see* radio; television
Broadcasting Council for Wales, 97
Brooke, Henry (now Baron Brooke of Cumnor), 105

Bryncroes, closing of school, 19
*Buchedd Garmon* (Lewis), 77
Builth Wells, 128
Burke, Edmund, 3
Burton, Richard, 136
*Bwrdd Croeso i Gymru* (Wales Welcome Board), 13

Caernarvon, 139; investiture of Prince of Wales, 23, 66, 88, 110, 111, 113–14, 199, 120, 134–5, 160
Caernarvonshire, Welsh teaching in, 65
Caerphilly, by-election (1968), 151
Cambrian Recordings, 69
Campbell, Sir Malcolm, 138
Capel Celyn, drowning of, 102, 104
Cardiff, 138–9; Polyphonic choir, 44; Welsh teaching in, 65; Tiger Bay, 138–9; as capital of Wales, 139
Cardiganshire: Welsh teaching in, 65, 95; and bilingual road signs, 89, 99; development association, 174
*Carlo* (Iwan), 88
Carmarthen: *Plaid Cymru* election success (1966), 150–1; defeat (1970), 152, 153
Carmarthenshire, 2, 137–8; Welsh teaching in, 65, 92; land reclamation, 179
*Celtic Nationalism* (Evans and Rhys), 164
chapels, 2, 16–17, 42–3, 53, 92, 129, 140
characteristics, 12–15
Charles, Prince, investiture of, 23, 66, 86, 88, 110, 111, 114, 134–5, 160
choral singing, 16, 41–4
Christian names, 5, 32
Cilmeri, 14, 88
classlessness, relative, 12, 15, 17
clubs, 18

191

public houses, Sunday opening of, 17-18
publishing, 60, 71-2
Pwllheli, *Plaid Cymru* founded at, 148

*Radical*, 157
radio, 54, 60, 69, 71; and Welsh language, 96-7
Radnorshire: little Welsh teaching in, 65; development association, 174
reclamation, 2, 139, 177-83
religion, 2, 15-18, 53
reservoirs, and threat to valleys, 102-8, 162
Rhayader, 174
Rhondda, 2, 139-43, 165; Pendyrus choir, 44; Welsh language in, 53, 140; mining, 140, 141, 146, 168, 181-2; community spirit, 141; depression in, 141-3; development plan, 182-3
Rhondda West, by-election (1967), 151
Rhys, Ioan, 164
Richards, Elwyn, and bilingual education project, 62, 63
road signs, campaign for bilingual, 22, 86, 89-91, 94-6, 98-9, 157
Rogers, Alun, 179
Rowlands, Ted, 162-3
Royal Air Force, bombing school, 75-6
Royal Mint, 127
Royal National *Eisteddfod*, 18, 34
Rugby football, 3, 7
Russell, Bertrand, 131, 133

*Saesneg* (English), 5, 49
St David's Day, 7-8
Schools Council, 63, 65
Secretary of State for Wales, post of, 161-3
*seisnigrwydd* (anglicization), 185
self-government, 148, 149, 154, 155, 161
Senni valley, 107
Severn River Authority, 106
Shaw, Bernard, 133
sheep, 5, 143-4
Simon, Dr Glyn, 90

singing, 16, 38, 41-4, 67-9, 87, 93-4
Skidmore, Ian, 120
society, 12, 15, 51
South Wales, 24; mining, 31, 53, 140, 166-70, 180; Independent Labour Party in, 147; industrial transformation, 165-75; unemployment and depopulation, 172-4; diversification, 175; land reclamation, 177-83; beauty of, 181
*South Wales Echo*, 61
South Wales Miners' Federation, 146
steel industry, 175
Sully, protesters at bilingual education project, 61
Sunday Closing Act, 18
surnames, 26, 28-32
Swansea: Welsh teaching in, 65; trial of language society leaders, 94-6

Taylor, George Francis, 119
television, 10, 18, 22, 54, 60, 68-71; and Welsh language, 96-8, 99-100, 185; and party political broadcasts, 152-3
Thomas, Dylan, 44, 136
Thomas, George, as Secretary for Wales, 22, 89, 161
Thomas, Gwyn, 55
Thomas, J. G. Parry, 138
Thomas, John, 45-6
Thomas, Mrs Mary, speaker of Welsh only, 47, 48-9
Thomas, Ned, 94-5
Tiger Bay, Cardiff, 138-9
Tolkien, J. R. R., 49
Tonypandy, 140, 141
tourism, 175
trade unionism, 53, 146
Transport, Ministry of, 85, 87, 162
Tremadoc Bay, 131
Treorchi, 140
Tryweryn dam, 92, 102-6, 108, 112
Tudur, Gwilym, 94, 95
*Tynged yr Iaith* (Lewis's 1962 radio lecture), 73, 79-82

*Under Milk Wood* (Thomas), 44, 136
unemployment, 141-3, 155, 158, 163, 167, 172-3